THE KEY

STUDENT STUDY GUIDE

Math 3

THE KEY student study guide is designed to help students achieve success in school. The content in each study guide is 100% curriculum aligned and serves as an excellent source of material for review and practice. To create this book, teachers, curriculum specialists, and assessment experts have worked closely to develop the instructional pieces that explain each of the key concepts for the course. The practice questions and sample tests have detailed solutions that show problem-solving methods, highlight concepts that are likely to be tested, and point out potential sources of errors. ***THE KEY*** is a complete guide to be used by students throughout the school year for reviewing and understanding course content, and to prepare for assessments.

Rao, Gautam, 1961 –
THE KEY – Math 3 Alberta

1. Mathematics – Juvenile Literature. I. Title

Castle Rock Research Corporation
2340 Manulife Place
10180 – 101 Street
Edmonton, AB T5J 3S4

2 3 4 FP 13 12 11

Publisher
Gautam Rao

Contributors
Robin Hobal
Phyllis Kozak

Reviewers
Allison Finch

Dedicated to the memory of Dr. V. S. Rao

THE KEY—Math 3

THE KEY consists of the following sections:

KEY Tips for Being Successful at School gives examples of study and review strategies. It includes information about learning styles, study schedules, and note taking for test preparation.

Class Focus includes a unit on each area of the curriculum. Units are divided into sections, each focusing on one of the specific expectations, or main ideas, that students must learn about in that unit. Examples, definitions, and visuals help to explain each main idea. Practice questions on the main ideas are also included. At the end of each unit is a test on the important ideas covered. The practice questions and unit tests help students identify areas they know and those they need to study more. They can also be used as preparation for tests and quizzes. Most questions are of average difficulty, though some are easy and some are hard. Each unit is prefaced by a **Table of Correlations**, which correlates questions in the unit to the specific curriculum expectations. Answers and solutions are found at the end of each unit.

KEY Strategies for Success on Tests helps students get ready for tests. It shows students different types of questions they might see, word clues to look for when reading them, and hints for answering them.

Practice Tests includes one to three tests based on the entire course. They are very similar to the format and level of difficulty that students may encounter on final tests. In some regions, these tests may be reprinted versions of official tests, or reflect the same difficulty levels and formats as official versions. This gives students the chance to practice using real-world examples. Answers and complete solutions are provided at the end of the section.

For the complete curriculum document (including specific expectations along with examples and sample problems), visit http://education.alberta.ca/media/645598/kto9math_ind.pdf.

THE KEY Study Guides are available for many courses. Check www.castlerockresearch.com for a complete listing of books available for your area.

For information about any of our resources or services, please call Castle Rock Research at 780.448.9619 or visit our website at http://www.castlerockresearch.com.

At Castle Rock Research, we strive to produce an error-free resource. If you should find an error, please contact us so that future editions can be corrected.

CONTENTS

KEY Tips for Being Successful in School

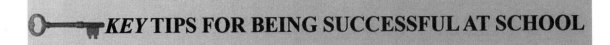

KEY TIPS FOR BEING SUCCESSFUL AT SCHOOL

KEY FACTORS CONTRIBUTING TO SCHOOL SUCCESS

In addition to learning the content of your courses, there are some other things that you can do to help you do your best at school. Some of these strategies are listed below.

- **Keep a positive attitude:** Always reflect on what you can already do and what you already know.

- **Be prepared to learn**: Have ready the necessary pencils, pens, notebooks, and other required materials for participating in class.

- **Complete all of your assignments:** Do your best to finish all of your assignments. Even if you know the material well, practice will reinforce your knowledge. If an assignment or question is difficult for you, work through it as far as you can so that your teacher can see exactly where you are having difficulty.

- **Set small goals for yourself when you are learning new material:** For example, when learning the parts of speech, do not try to learn everything in one night. Work on only one part or section each study session. When you have memorized one particular part of speech and understand it, then move on to another one, continue this process until you have memorized and learned all the parts of speech.

- **Review your classroom work regularly at home:** Review to be sure that you understand the material that you learned in class.

- **Ask your teacher for help**: Your teacher will help you if you do not understand something or if you are having a difficult time completing your assignments.

- **Get plenty of rest and exercise:** Concentrating in class is hard work. It is important to be well-rested and have time to relax and socialize with your friends. This helps you to keep your positive attitude about your school work.

- **Eat healthy meals:** A balanced diet keeps you healthy and gives you the energy that you need for studying at school and at home.

HOW TO FIND YOUR LEARNING STYLE

Every student learns differently. The manner in which you learn best is called your learning style. By knowing your learning style, you can increase your success at school. Most students use a combination of learning styles. Do you know what type of learner you are? Read the following descriptions. Which of these common learning styles do you use most often?

• **Do you need to say things out loud?** You may learn best by saying, hearing, and seeing words. You are probably really good at memorizing things such as dates, places, names, and facts. You may need **to write and then say out loud** the steps in a process, a formula, or the actions that lead up to a significant event.

• **Do you need to read or see things?** You may learn best by looking at and working with pictures. You are probably really good at puzzles, imagining things, and reading maps and charts. You may need to use strategies like **mind mapping and webbing** to organize your information and study notes.

• **Do you need to draw or write things down?** You may learn best by touching, moving, and figuring things out using manipulatives. You are probably really good at physical activities and learning through movement. You may need to **draw your finger over a diagram** to remember it, **"tap out" the steps** needed to solve a problem, or **"feel" yourself writing or typing** a formula.

SCHEDULING STUDY TIME

You should review your class notes regularly to ensure that you have a clear understanding of all the new material you learned. Reviewing your lessons on a regular basis helps you to learn and remember ideas and concepts. It also reduces the quantity of material that you need to study prior to a test. Establishing a study schedule will help you to make the best use of your time.

Regardless of the type of study schedule you use, you may want to consider the following suggestions to maximize your study time and effort:

- Organize your work so that you begin with the most challenging material first.
- Divide the subject's content into small, manageable chunks.
- Alternate regularly between your different subjects and types of study activities in order to maintain your interest and motivation.
- Make a daily list with headings like "Must Do," "Should Do," and "Could Do."
- Begin each study session by quickly reviewing what you studied the day before.
- Maintain your usual routine of eating, sleeping, and exercising to help you concentrate better for extended periods of time.

MIND-MAPPING OR WEBBING

Use the key words, ideas, or concepts from your reading or class notes to create a *mind map* or *web* (a diagram or visual representation of the given information). A mind map or web is sometimes referred to as a knowledge map.

- Write the key word, concept, theory, or formula in the centre of your page.

- Write down related facts, ideas, events, and information and then link them to the central concept with lines.

- Use coloured markers, underlining, or other symbols to emphasize things such as relationships, time lines, and important information.

- The following examples of a Frayer Model illustrate how this technique can be used to study scientific vocabulary.

Definition – Perimeter is the distance around a polygon	**Characteristics** – Measured in linear units (e.g., metres, centimetres)	**Definition** A cube is a solid 3-D object that has – 6 square faces, all equal in size – 8 vertices – 12 equal edges	**Visual Presentation**
Perimeter		**Cube**	
Examples – Fence around a yard – Distance around a circle (circumference)	**Non-examples** – Grass covering a yard – Area of rug covering a floor	**Characteristics or Properties** – 6 square faces – 8 vertices – 12 edges – 6 flat faces	**Examples**

INDEX CARDS

To use index cards while studying, follow these steps:

- Write a key word or question on one side of an index card.

- On the reverse side, write the definition of the word, answer to the question, or any other important information that you want to remember.

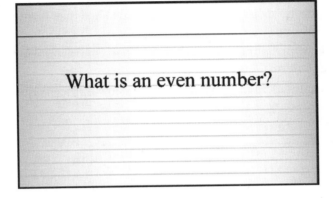

SYMBOLS AND STICKY NOTES—IDENTIFYING IMPORTANT INFORMATION

- Use symbols to mark your class notes. For example, an exclamation mark (!) might be used to point out something that must be learned well because it is a very important idea. A question mark (?) may highlight something that you are not certain about, and a diamond (◊) or asterisk (*) could highlight interesting information that you want to remember.

- Use sticky notes when you are not allowed to put marks in books.

- Use sticky notes to mark a page in a book that contains an important diagram, formula, explanation, etc.

- Use sticky notes to mark important facts in research books.

MEMORIZATION TECHNIQUES

- **Association** relates new learning to something you already know. For example, to remember the spelling difference between *dessert* and *desert*, recall that the word *sand* has only one *s*. So, because there is sand in a desert, the word *desert* only has on *s*.

- **Mnemonic** devices are sentences that you create to remember a list or group of items. For example, the first letter of each word in the phrase "Every Good Boy Deserves Fudge" helps you to remember the names of the lines on the treble clef staff (E, G, B, D, and F) in music.

- **Acronyms** are words that are formed from the first letters or parts of the words in a group. For example, **RADAR** is actually an acronym for **Ra**dio **D**etecting **A**nd **R**anging, and **MASH** is an acronym for **M**obile **A**rmy **S**urgical **H**ospital. **HOMES** helps you to remember the names of the five Great Lakes (**H**uron, **O**ntario, **M**ichigan, **E**rie, and **S**uperior).

- **Visualizing** requires you to use your mind's eye to "see" a chart, list, map, diagram, or sentence as it is in your textbook or notes, on the chalk board or computer screen, or in a display.

- **Initialisms** are abbreviations that are formed from the first letters or parts of the words in a group. Unlike acronyms, initialisms cannot be pronounced as a word themselves. For example, **BEDMAS** is an initialism for the order of operations in math (**B**rackets, **E**xponents, **D**ivide, **M**ultiply, **A**dd, **S**ubtract).

KEY STRATEGIES FOR REVIEWING

Reviewing textbook material, class notes, and handouts should be an ongoing activity. Spending time reviewing becomes more critical when you are preparing for tests. You may find some of the following review strategies useful when studying during your scheduled study time.

- Before reading a selection, preview it by noting the headings, charts, graphs, and chapter questions.
- Highlight mathematical key concepts, vocabulary, definitions, and formulas.
- Carefully read over each step in a procedure.
- Draw a picture or diagram to help make the concept clearer.

KEY STRATEGIES FOR SUCCESS: A CHECKLIST

Review, review, review: review is a huge part of doing well at school and preparing for tests. Here is a checklist for you to keep track of how many suggested strategies for success you are using. Read each question and then put a check mark (✓) in the correct column. Look at the questions where you have checked the "No" column. Think about how you might try using some of these strategies to help you do your best at school.

KEY Strategies for Success	Yes	No
Do you attend school regularly?		
Do you know your personal learning style—how you learn best?		
Do you spend 15 to 30 minutes a day reviewing your notes?		
Do you study in a quiet place at home?		
Do you clearly mark the most important ideas in your study notes?		
Do you use sticky notes to mark texts and research books?		
Do you practise answering multiple-choice and written-response questions?		
Do you ask your teacher for help when you need it?		
Are you maintaining a healthy diet and sleep routine?		
Are you participating in regular physical activity?		

Number

NUMBER

Table of Correlations

Outcome		Practice Questions	Unit Test Questions	Practice Test
3N1.0	Develop number sense.			
3N1.1	Say the number sequence 0 to 1000 forward and backward.	1, 2	1	1
3N1.2	Represent and describe numbers to 1000, concretely, pictorially and symbolically.	3, 4, 5	2, 3, 4	2, 3
3N1.3	Compare and order numbers to 1000.	6, 7	5	4
3N1.4	Estimate quantities less than 1000, using referents.	8, 9	6	5
3N1.5	Illustrate, concretely and pictorially, the meaning of place value for numerals to 1000.	10, 11, 12	7, 8	6, 7
3N1.6	Describe and apply mental mathematics strategies for adding two 2-digit numerals.	13, 14	9	8
3N1.7	Describe and apply mental mathematics strategies for subtracting two 2-digit numerals.	15, 16	10	9
3N1.8	Apply estimation strategies to predict sums and differences of two 2-digit numerals in a problem-solving context.	17, 18	11	10
3N1.9	Demonstrate an understanding of addition and subtraction of numbers with answers to 1000, concretely, pictorially and symbolically.	19, 20	12, 13	11
3N1.10	Apply mental mathematics strategies and number properties.	21, 22	14	12
3N1.11	Demonstrate an understanding of multiplication to 5 × 5.	23, 24	15	13
3N1.12	Demonstrate an understanding of division.	25, 26	16	14
3N1.13	Demonstrate an understanding of fractions.	27, 28, 29	17, 18	15, 16

3N1.1 *Say the number sequence 0 to 1000 forward and backward.*

COUNTING

You can count forward or backward from any starting point.

COUNTING FORWARD

To count forward, add the same given number over and over. Look for patterns that can help you.

You can use any starting point:

- To count by 5s, add 5 to each number. For example, 8, 13, 18, 23, …
- To count by 10s, add 10 to each number. For example, 12, 22, 32, …
- To count by 100s, add 100 to each number. For example, 102, 202, 302, …

You can use starting points that are multiples of a given number:

- To count by 3s, add 3 to each number. For example, 3, 6, 9, …
- To count by 4s, add 4 to each number. For example, 4, 8, 12, …
- To count by 25s, add 25 to each number. For example, 25, 50, 75, 100, …

Example

Skip count by 4s from 88 to 104.

Solution

Start at 88, and add 4 to each number to get the next number.
88, 92, 96, 100, 104

COUNTING BACKWARD

To count backward, subtract the same given number over and over. Look for patterns that can help you.

You can use any starting point:

- To count backward by 5s, subtract 5 from each number.
  For example, 27, 22, 17, 12, …
- To count backward by 10s, subtract 10 from each number.
  For example, 189, 179, 169, …
- To count backward by 100s, subtract 100 from each number.
  For example, 915, 815, 715, …

You can use starting points that are multiples of a given number:

- To count backward by 3s, subtract 3 from each number. For example, 24, 21, 18, ...
- To count backward by 4s, subtract 4 from each number. For example, 28, 24, 20, ...
- To count backward by 25s, subtract 25 from each number. For example, 275, 250, 225, ...

Example

Skip count backward by 100s from 433 to 33.

Solution

Start with 433, and subtract 100 from each number to get the next number.
433, 333, 233, 133, 33

When skip counting by 100, the numbers in the ones and tens places do not change.

COUNTING USING COINS

To skip count using coins, choose a number as a starting point, and then add the same number over and over. Look for patterns that can help you.

- When using nickels, add 5¢ to each number. For example, 5¢, 10¢, 15¢,...
- When using dimes, add 10¢ to each number. For example, 10¢, 20¢, 30¢,...
- When using quarters, add 25¢ to each number. For example, 25¢, 50¢, 75¢,...
- When using loonies, add $1 to each number. For example, $1, $2, $3,...

Example

Stewart has 5 quarters in his pocket.

How much money does he have?

Solution

One quarter is worth 25 ¢. Count by 25s for each quarter.
25, 50, 75, 100, 125

Stewart has 125 ¢, or $1.25.

Use the following information to answer the next question.

Megan skip counts backward from 791 seven times and ends at 721.

1. What number was Megan skip counting by to get from 791 to 721?
   A. 2 B. 5
   C. 10 D. 100

Use the following information to answer the next question.

Gilbert makes four piles of coins.

- One pile has 33 pennies.
- One pile has 22 nickels.
- One pile has 15 dimes.
- One pile has 11 quarters.

2. Which pile of coins has the **greatest** value?
   A. Dimes   B. Nickels
   C. Pennies   D. Quarters

3N1.2 Represent and describe numbers to 1000, concretely, pictorially and symbolically.

REPRESENTING AND DESCRIBING NUMBERS TO 1 000

You can represent numbers concretely, pictorially, and symbolically.

SHOWING NUMBERS USING BASE TEN BLOCKS

The base ten blocks are called units, ten rods, and hundred flats.

- A unit has a value of 1.

- A ten rod has a value of 10. It is made up of 10 units.

- A hundred flat has a value of 100. It is made up of 10 ten rods or 100 units.

You can use base ten blocks to build numbers. You can also draw base ten blocks to show numbers.

Example

Using the fewest base ten blocks, build the number 251.

Solution

Step 1
Figure out the number of hundreds, tens, and ones in the number.

In 251, there are 2 hundreds, 5 tens, and 1 one.

Step 2
Show the hundreds, tens, and ones with base ten blocks.

To show 2 hundreds, use 2 hundred flats.

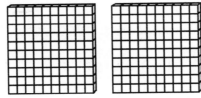

To show 5 tens, use 5 ten rods.

To show 1 one, use 1 unit.

Step 3
Put the blocks together.

Using the fewest base ten blocks, the number 251 is shown with these blocks.

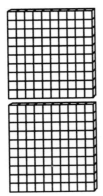

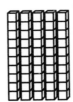

USING EXPRESSIONS

An expression can be used to show a number in a different way. An expression does not use an equal sign (=).

- An expression can be the sum of two numbers. For example, 500 can be shown as 200 + 300.
- An expression can be the difference between two numbers. For example, 500 can be shown as 600 – 100.

Example

Using an expression, show the number 450 in two ways.

Solution

Step 1

Use addition.

One way to show 450 is to add the 4 hundreds (400) and the 5 tens (50). The number 450 is shown as 400 + 50.

Step 2

Use subtraction.

One way to show 450 is to subtract 50 from 500. The number 450 is shown as 500 – 50.

READING AND WRITING NUMBERS

When reading three-digit numbers, read from left to right. Say the number of the hundreds, followed by the word *hundred*. Then, say the tens and the ones as a unit. For example, to read 732, say "seven hundred thirty-two."

WRITING MULTIPLES OF 10

To write multiples of 10, the words from two to five change their spelling and end in *-ty*.

- two → twenty
- three → thirty
- four → forty
- five → fifty

The words from six to nine use the same spelling and end in *-ty*.

- six → sixty
- seven → seventy
- eight → eighty
- nine → ninety

Example

Write the number 40 as a word.

Solution

The number 40 is a multiple of 10. The spelling of four (4) changes when the multiple of 10 is written.

Drop the *u* in four, and add *-ty* to the end of the word.

four → forty

WRITING MULTIPLES OF 100

To write multiples of 100, use the words one to nine followed by the word *hundred*.

- one → one hundred
- two → two hundred
- three → three hundred

Use the following information to answer the next question.

Kyle uses these base ten blocks to show a number.

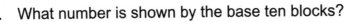

3. What number is shown by the base ten blocks?

   A. 28   B. 108

   C. 198   D. 208

4. Written in words, what multiple of 100 comes before 600?

   A. Six hundred   B. Five hundred

   C. Fifty hundred   D. Seventy hundred

5. Using the fewest base ten blocks, build the number 437.

3N1.3 Compare and order numbers to 1000.

ORDERING NUMBERS

Numbers can be ordered from least to greatest (ascending order). For example, 345, 450, and 492.

Numbers can also be ordered from greatest to least (descending order). For example, 492, 450, and 345.

You can use hundred charts, place values, or number lines to help you order given numbers.

USING HUNDRED CHARTS

A hundred chart writes the numbers in order from 1 to 100.

Example

A hundred chart is given.

1	2	3	4	5	6	7	8	9	10
11	12	13	14	15	16	17	18	19	20
21	22	23	24	25	26	27	28	29	30
31	32	33	34	35	36	37	38	39	40
41	42	43	44	45	46	47	48	49	50
51	52	53	54	55	56	57	58	59	60
61	62	63	64	65	66	67	68	69	70
71	72	73	74	75	76	77	78	79	80
81	82	83	84	85	86	87	88	89	90
91	92	93	94	95	96	97	98	99	100

Use a hundred chart to order the numbers 37, 73, 55, 64, and 46 from greatest to least.

Solution

Step 1
Shade all the given numbers on the hundred chart.

1	2	3	4	5	6	7	8	9	10
11	12	13	14	15	16	17	18	19	20
21	22	23	24	25	26	27	28	29	30
31	32	33	34	35	36	37	38	39	40
41	42	43	44	45	46	47	48	49	50
51	52	53	54	55	56	57	58	59	60
61	62	63	64	65	66	67	68	69	70
71	72	73	74	75	76	77	78	79	80
81	82	83	84	85	86	87	88	89	90
91	92	93	94	95	96	97	98	99	100

Step 2
Write the shaded numbers in the order they are shown, starting with the greatest number (73).

From greatest to least, the numbers are 73, 64, 55, 46, and 37.

USING PLACE VALUE

Place value can be used to compare and order numbers. By looking at the digits in each place value position, you will be able to order numbers.

Start with the greatest place value position (hundreds), and work toward the least place value position (ones). Always move from left to right. The number that has the largest digit in the hundreds is the greatest number.

If two or more numbers have the same number of hundreds, move to the right, and compare the tens. If two or more numbers have the same number of tens, compare the ones.

Example

List the numbers 442, 486, 323, and 502 in order from the greatest value to the least value.

Solution

Step 1
Write the numbers below each other, lining up the place values.

442

486

323

502

Step 2
Compare the hundreds.
442
486
323
502

Since 5 is greater than 4 and 3, the number 502 has the greatest value.

Since 3 is less than 4 and 5, the number 323 has the least value.

Step 3
Compare the tens place for 442 and 486.
442
486

Since 8 is greater than 4, the number 486 is greater than the number 442.

Step 4
Order the numbers from greatest value to least value.

From greatest to least, the numbers are 502, 486, 442, and 323.

USING NUMBER LINES

A number line starts with one number and ends with a larger number. Some number lines are broken into equal parts. You order numbers on a number line by writing them between the labelled numbers. A number line can also be used to check the order of a given set of numbers.

Example

Use a number line to order the numbers 759, 767, 751, and 763 from least to greatest.

Solution

Step 1
Show the numbers from least to greatest.

From least to greatest, the numbers are 751, 759, 763, and 767.

Step 2
Order the numbers on a number line.

Start your number line at 750, and end it at 770. Break the number line into equal parts. Count by 5s.
750, 755, 760, 765, 770

The numbers are shown in order on this number line.

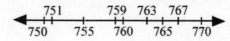

Written Response

6. Order the numbers 565, 595, and 580 by placing them on this number line.

550   600

Written Response

7. Order the numbers 818, 955, and 839 from greatest value to least value.

3N1.4 Estimate quantities less than 1000, using referents.

ESTIMATING USING REFERENTS

When you estimate, you give your best guess, not the actual answer.

One way to make an estimate for a large number of objects is to use a referent. A referent can be a small group with a particular number of objects in it that can be used to estimate a larger group of objects.

USING 10 AS A REFERENT

Using a number like 10 as a referent makes it easier to count when you are estimating a larger number of objects. For example, to estimate a large number of items, draw a ring around 10 of the items. Then, draw rings around the rest of the items, making groups that look like there are about 10 items in each group. Count the number of groups you made by 10s to get an estimate of the total number.

Example

Wendy's teacher asks her to estimate the number of stars in this picture.

Show how Wendy could use a referent of 10 to estimate the number of stars.

Solution

Step 1

Use a referent of 10.

Count out a group of 10 stars to use as a referent. Draw a ring around the 10 stars. Make groups of stars that look like they could have about 10 stars in each group.

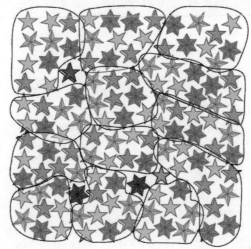

Step 2
Estimate the number of stars.
There are two ways to make the estimate.

1. Count by tens for each group made.
   10, 20, 30, 40, 50, 60, 70, 80, 90, 100, 110, 120, 130
2. Count the number of groups made, and multiply that number by 10. To multiply by 10, add one zero to the end of the number of groups.
   13 groups × 1<u>0</u> = 13<u>0</u>

A good estimate is that there are about 130 stars in the picture.

USING 100 AS A REFERENT

To estimate using 100 as a referent, count the number of hundreds in the given number. Then, count up to the next hundred. Figure out which hundred is closest to the given number.

Example
  There are 593 straws in a box that holds 1 000 straws.

  Using 100 as a referent, about how many straws are in the box?

Solution
  ## Step 1
  Count the number of hundreds in 593.
  100, 200, 300, 400, 500

  ## Step 2
  Count up to the next hundred.
  100, 200, 300, 400, 500, 600
  The number 593 is between 500 and 600.

  ## Step 3
  Figure out which hundred is closer to 593.
  Count by tens.
  500, 510, 520, 530, 540, 550, 560, 570, 580, **590, 600**
  The number 593 is closer to 600.
  A good estimate is that there are about 600 straws in the box.

Use the following information to answer the next question.

Ellen collected 736 pennies for an animal shelter.

8. Using the referent of 100 pennies = $1.00, the **best** estimate of the amount of money Ellen collected is

A. $5.00   B. $6.00

C. $7.00   D. $8.00

Use the following information to answer the next question.

Jenna sees this design of stars in her math textbook.

Written Response

9. What would be a good estimate of the number of stars in the design?

3N1.5 Illustrate, concretely and pictorially, the meaning of place value for numerals to 1000.

PLACE VALUE

Where a digit is placed in a number tells you the value of the digit.

- A digit in the ones place has a value of 1.
- A digit in the tens place has a value of 10.
- A digit in the hundreds place has a value of 100.

SHOWING PLACE VALUE WITH BASE TEN BLOCKS

You can show the place value of each digit in a number by using base ten blocks.
For example, the number 132 can be shown as 1 hundred flat, 3 ten rods, and 2 units.

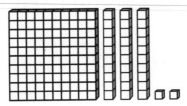

- The value of 1 hundred flat is 100.
- The value of 3 ten rods is 30.
- The value of 2 units is 2.
  100 + 30 + 2 = 132

You can show the same number in more than one way by using different sets of base ten blocks. For example, the number 132 can also be shown with 1 hundred flat, 2 ten rods, and 12 units.

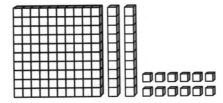

- The value of 1 hundred flat is 100.
- The value of 2 ten rods is 20.
- The value of 12 units is 12.
  100 + 20 + 12 = 132

Example

Using base ten blocks, show the values of each digit in the number 215. Show the place values in two ways.

Solution

Step 1
Figure out the place value of each digit.

- The digit 2 has a value of 200.
- The digit 1 has a value of 10.
- The digit 5 has a value of 5.

Step 2
Show the values with the fewest number of blocks.

- Use 2 hundred flats to show 200.
- Use 1 ten rod to show 10.
- Use 5 units to show 5.

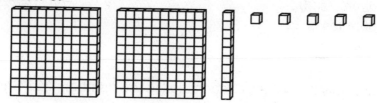

This equals 200 + 10 + 5 = 215.

Step 3
Show the values with a different set of blocks.

The number 215 can also be shown with 1 hundred flat, 11 tens, and 5 ones.

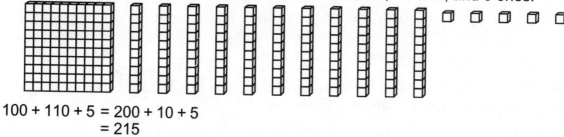

$$100 + 110 + 5 = 200 + 10 + 5$$
$$= 215$$

USING MONEY TO SHOW PLACE VALUE

You can show the place value of each digit in a three-digit number by using loonies ($1 or 100¢), dimes (10¢), and pennies (1¢).

- 1 penny = 1 unit (1)
- 1 dime = 1 ten rod (10)
- 1 loonie = 1 hundred flat (100)

For example, the number 123 can be represented using 1 loonie, 2 dimes, and 3 pennies.

The value of 1 loonie is 100¢.
The value of 2 dimes is 20¢.
The value of 3 pennies is 3¢.
100 + 20 + 3 = 123

Example

Using money, show the values of each digit in the number 432. Show the place values in two ways.

Solution

Step 1
Determine the place value of each digit.

- The digit 4 has a value of 400.
- The digit 3 has a value of 30.
- The digit 2 has a value of 2.

Step 2
Show the values with the fewest number of coins.

- Use 4 loonies to show 400.
- Use 3 dimes to show 30.
- Use 2 pennies to show 2.

This equals 400 + 30 + 2 = 432.

Step 3
Show the values with a different set of coins.
The number 432 can also be shown with 4 loonies, 2 dimes, and 12 pennies.

26

ZERO AS A PLACEHOLDER

When writing a number that is shown in base ten blocks or money, it is important to write a zero if a place value is not shown.

Example

Base ten blocks show the value of each digit in a number.

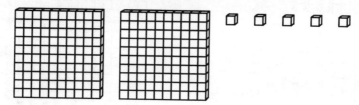

Write the number shown.

Solution

Step 1

Write the hundreds digit.

There are 2 hundred flats. They have a value of 200. Write the digit 2.

2_ _

Step 2

Write the tens digit.

There are no tens shown. Write 0 to the right of the 2 to act as a placeholder.

20_

Step 3

Write the ones digit.

There are 5 units. Write a 5 to the right of the 0.

205

The number shown by the base ten blocks is 205.

It is important to write the 0 as a placeholder. If you did not write the 0, the number would be 25, which is very different from 205.

Use the following information to answer the next question.

The base ten blocks show the value of each digit in a number.

10. What is the number shown?

A. 35

B. 53

C. 305

D. 350

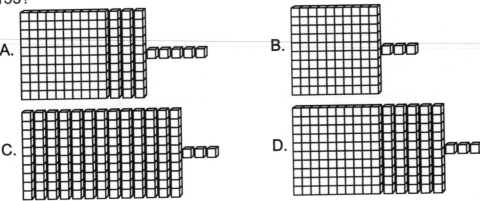

11. Which set of base ten blocks show the place value of each digit in the number 153?

A.

B.

C.

D.

12. Which of the following sets of coins shows the place value of each digit in the number 252?

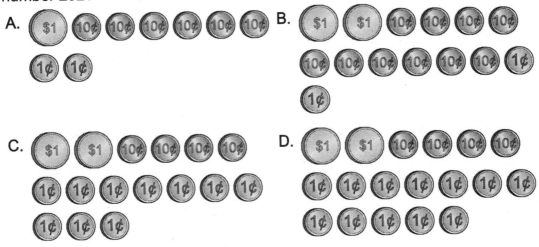

A. $1 10¢ 10¢ 10¢ 10¢ 10¢ 10¢ 1¢ 1¢

B. $1 $1 10¢ 10¢ 10¢ 10¢ 10¢ 10¢ 10¢ 10¢ 10¢ 10¢ 1¢ 1¢

C. $1 $1 10¢ 10¢ 10¢ 10¢ 1¢ 1¢ 1¢ 1¢ 1¢ 1¢ 1¢ 1¢ 1¢ 1¢

D. $1 $1 10¢ 10¢ 10¢ 10¢ 1¢ 1¢ 1¢ 1¢ 1¢ 1¢ 1¢ 1¢ 1¢ 1¢ 1¢ 1¢

3N1.6 Describe and apply mental mathematics strategies for adding two 2-digit numerals.

ADDING WITH MENTAL MATH

Using mental math when you add means you are adding the numbers in your head.

Here are some strategies to help you add quickly in your head. In each strategy, you are using numbers that are easier to work with.

ADDING FROM LEFT TO RIGHT

To add from left to right, think of breaking the numbers into their tens and ones. First, add the tens of both numbers. Then, add the ones of both numbers. Then, add the tens and the ones together.

Example

Add 34 + 16 in your head by adding from left to right.

Solution

Step 1
For each number, break them into tens and ones.
Think of 34 as 30 + 4 and 16 as 10 + 6.

Step 2
Add the tens of both numbers together, and add the ones of both numbers together.
Add the tens.
30 + 10 = 40
Add the ones.
4 + 6 = 10

Step 3
Add the tens and the ones together.
40 + 10 = 50
This means the answer is 34 + 16 = 50.

MAKING A ZERO

To use the strategy of making a zero, make one of the numbers end in zero.

Follow these steps to make a zero:

1. Start with the number that is closest to a multiple of 10, and make that number end in zero.
2. Add the two numbers.
3. Whatever number you added or subtracted to make the number end in zero, do the opposite to the number you find.

Example

Add 39 + 46 in your head by making a zero.

Solution

Step 1
Start with the number that is closest to a multiple of 10, and make that number end in zero.
Think of 39 as 40(39 + 1 = 40).

Step 2
Add the two numbers.
40 + 46 = 86

Step 3

Whatever number you added or subtracted to make the number end in zero, do the opposite to the number you find.

Since you added 1 to 39, subtract 1 from 86.

86 − 1 = 85

The answer is 39 + 46 = 85.

You can also think of this as one step.

To add 39 + 46, think 40 + 46 − 1 = 85.

MAKING DOUBLES

Sometimes, doubles are easier to add in your head than other numbers. Usually you can use the strategy of doubles when you have a math problem where the numbers are almost doubles. To make doubles, you add the same number to itself.

Follow these steps to add numbers using doubles:

1. Change one of the numbers so that the two numbers being added are the same.
2. Add the two numbers.
3. Whatever operation you used in step 1, do the opposite to the answer you find.

Example

Add 14 + 16 in your head by using doubles.

Solution

Step 1

Change one of the numbers so that the two numbers being added are the same.

Think of 14 + 16 as 14 + 14.

Step 2

Add the two numbers.

14 + 14 = 28

Step 3

Whatever operation you used in step 1, do the opposite to the answer you find.

Since you subtracted 2 from 16, add 2 to 28.

28 + 2 = 30

The answer is 14 + 16 = 30.

You can also think of this as one step.

To add 14 + 16, think 14 + 14 + 2 = 30.

Use the following information to answer the next question.

Sandra and Jenny sold candy bars for a fundraiser. Sandra sold 41 candy bars, and Jenny sold 56 candy bars.

13. Which of the following strategies shows a quick way of adding 41 + 56?
    A. Add the sum of 4 + 1 to the sum of 5 + 6.
    B. Add the sum of 4 + 5 to the sum of 1 + 6.
    C. Add the sum of 40 + 60 to the sum of 1 + 5.
    D. Add the sum of 40 + 50 to the sum of 1 + 6.

14. Jason has 19 toy cars and 15 toy trucks. A quick method to find the total number of toys Jason has is to
    A. add the sum of 20 + 1 to the sum of 9 + 5
    B. add the sum of 1 + 1 to the sum of 9 + 5
    C. subtract 1 from the sum of 20 + 15
    D. subtract 1 from the sum of 19 + 15

3N1.7   Describe and apply mental mathematics strategies for subtracting two 2-digit numerals.

SUBTRACTING WITH MENTAL MATH STRATEGIES

Using mental math when you subtract means you subtract the numbers in your head.

These are some strategies to help you subtract numbers quickly in your head. In each strategy, you are using numbers that are easier to work with.

ADDING ON

To use the strategy of adding on, think of counting up from the smaller number to the larger number.

Follow these steps to use adding on:

1. Start with the smaller number. Add on numbers that are easy to work with as you count up to the larger number.
2. Find the sum of the numbers you added on. The sum will be the answer to the subtraction problem.

Example

Subtract 84 – 67 in your head by using the strategy of adding on.

Solution

Step 1

Start with the smaller number.

The smaller number is 67. Add on numbers that are easy to work with as you count up to the larger number.

$67 + \boxed{3} = 70$

$70 + \boxed{10} = 80$

$80 + \boxed{4} = 84$

Step 2

Add the three numbers you added on.

$3 + 10 + 4 = 17$

The answer is $84 - 67 = 17$.

MAKING A ZERO

To use the strategy of making a zero, make the smaller number end in zero.

Follow these steps to make a zero:

1. Change the number being subtracted into the nearest multiple of 10.
2. Subtract the two numbers.
3. Perform the operation used in step 1 again on the answer you find.

Example

Subtract 54 – 29 in your head by making a zero.

Solution

Step 1

Change the number being subtracted into the nearest multiple of 10.

The number being subtracted is 29. Add 1 to make it the nearest multiple of 10.

$29 + 1 = 30$

Step 2

Subtract the two numbers.

Subtract 30 from 54.

$54 - 30 = 24$

Step 3

Perform the operation used in step 1 again on the answer you find.

Since you added 1 to 29, add 1 to 24.

$24 + 1 = 25$

The answer is $54 - 29 = 25$.

USING DOUBLES

To use the strategy of doubles, think of the smaller number as half the larger number. For example, to subtract 42 – 21, think of 21 + 21 = 42. Since 21 + 21 = 42, then 42 – 21 = 21.

Example

Subtract 72 – 36 in your head by using doubles.

Solution

The smaller number is 36. Double the number 36.
36 + 36 = 72

Since 36 + 36 = 72, then 72 – 36 = 36.

Use the following information to answer the next question.

On a trip to the lake, Lisa picks up 46 rocks. She throws 22 rocks into the lake.

15. The mental strategy Lisa could use to find out how many rocks she kept is to think
    A. 41 – 21 and 20 – 3
    B. 40 – 20 and 20 + 5
    C. 46 – 20 and 26 + 2
    D. 46 – 20 and 26 – 2

Use the following information to answer the next question.

Jesse used the strategy of adding on to solve the equation 51 – 38 = ☐.

16. Which of the following sets of equations shows how Jesse used the strategy of adding on?
    A. 38 – 8 = 30, 30 + 21 = 51
    B. 38 + 38 = 76, 76 – 51 = 25
    C. 38 + 2 = 40, 40 + 10 = 50,
       50 + 1 = 51
    D. 51 + 9 = 60, 38 + 20 = 58,
       58 + 2 = 60

3N1.8 Apply estimation strategies to predict sums and differences of two 2-digit numerals in a problem-solving context.

ESTIMATING TO SOLVE PROBLEMS

An estimate does not give an exact answer to a problem. An estimate gives an answer that is close to the exact answer.

USING FRONT-END ESTIMATION

One way to estimate is to keep the first digit of a two-digit number and replace the last digit with a zero. This is called front-end estimation.

For example, to estimate the difference of 63 – 25, use 60 – 20.

63 → 60

25 → 20

Subtract the two estimated numbers.

60 – 20 = 40

The difference of 63 – 25 is close to 40.

Example

At one school, 24 boys and 33 girls signed up for the running club.

Using front-end estimation, about how many students signed up for the running club?

Solution

Step 1

Keep the first digit of each two-digit number, and replace the last digit with a zero.

24 → 20

33 → 30

To estimate the sum of 24 + 33, use 20 + 30.

Step 2

Add the estimated numbers.

20 + 30 = 50

About 50 students signed up for the running club.

Use the following information to answer the next question.

Dani had 44 hair clips. She gave 17 of her hair clips to her younger sister.

17. Using front-end estimation, about how many hair clips does Dani have left?

A. 30

B. 27

C. 25

D. 20

Use the following information to answer the next question.

Zack has 45 nickles and 23 dimes in his money jar. He uses front-end estimation to figure out about how many coins he has altogether.

18. Which of the following estimates did Zack use?

A. 50 + 30 = 80

B. 50 + 20 = 70

C. 40 + 30 = 70

D. 40 + 20 = 60

3N1.9 Demonstrate an understanding of addition and subtraction of numbers with answers to 1000, concretely, pictorially and symbolically.

ADDING AND SUBTRACTING

You can use numbers or base ten blocks to add and subtract.

ADDITION USING BASE TEN BLOCKS

You can use base ten blocks to help you add numbers.

1. Build the two numbers you are adding.
2. Combine the blocks that have the same place value.
3. Regroup the blocks where needed.

Example

Use base ten blocks to add 214 + 368.

Solution

Step 1

Use base ten blocks to build each of the numbers.

Build the number 214. Use 2 hundred flats, 1 ten rod, and 4 units to show 214.

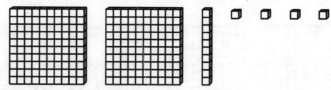

Build the number 368. Use 3 hundred flats, 6 ten rods, and 8 units to show 368.

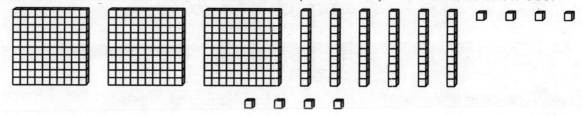

Step 2

Combine the blocks that have the same place values.

There are 5 hundred flats in all.

There are 7 ten rods in all.

There are 12 units in all.

Step 3

Regroup the units.

Only one digit is allowed in each place value position. Take 10 units, and exchange them for 1 rod.

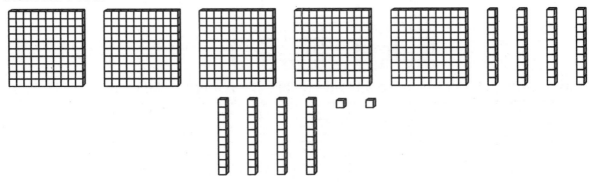

Now you have 5 hundred flats (500), 8 ten rods (80), and 2 units (2).

500 + 80 + 2 = 582

The answer is 214 + 368 = 582.

ADDITION USING NUMBERS

When adding numbers, write the numbers below each other, lining up the place values.

- Work from right to left. Add the digits in the ones place, then the tens place, and then the hundreds place.
- Regroup where needed.

Example

Show how to add 214 + 368 using numbers.

Solution

Step 1

Write the numbers below each other, lining up the place values.

```
 214
+368
```

Step 2

Add the ones.

$4 + 8 = 12$

You need to regroup the 12 ones into 1 ten and 2 ones.

$12 \rightarrow 10 + 2$

Write the 2 ones below the 4 and 8 in the ones place.

Write the 1 ten above the tens place.

```
  1
 214
+368
   2
```

Step 3

Add the tens.

$1 + 1 + 6 = 8$

Write the 8 below the line in the tens place.

```
  1
 214
+368
  82
```

Step 4

Add the hundreds.

$2 + 3 = 5$

Write the 5 below the line in the hundreds place.

```
  1
 214
+368
 582
```

The answer is $214 + 368 = 582$.

SUBTRACTION USING BASE TEN BLOCKS

You can use base ten blocks to help you subtract numbers.

1. Build the two numbers you are subtracting.
2. Starting at the units, take away the blocks you do not need.
3. Regroup the blocks where needed.

Example

Use base ten blocks to subtract 110 – 50.

Solution

Step 1

Use base ten blocks to build the two numbers.

Build the number 110.

Use 1 hundred flat and 1 ten rod.

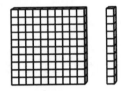

Build the number 50.

Use 5 ten rods.

Step 2

Regroup the tens.

You cannot take 5 tens away from 1 ten, so you need to regroup. The hundred flat can be regrouped into 10 ten rods.

Add the 10 ten rods to the 1 ten rod. You now have 11 ten rods.

Now, you can subtract 5 ten rods from 11 ted rods.

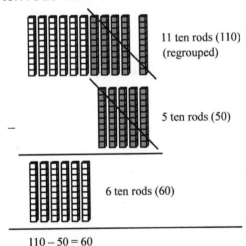

11 ten rods (110)
(regrouped)

5 ten rods (50)

6 ten rods (60)

110 – 50 = 60

The ten rods that are crossed out show that 5 ten rods (50) have been taken away from 11 ten rods (110). You are left with 6 ten rods (60).

The answer is 100 – 50 = 60.

SUBTRACTION USING NUMBERS

When subtracting numbers, write the numbers below each other, lining up the place values.

- Work from right to left. Subtract the bottom digit from the top digit in the ones place, then the tens place, and then the hundreds place.
- Regroup when the top digit is smaller than the bottom digit.

Example

Show how to subtract 110 – 50 using numbers.

Solution

Step 1

Write the numbers below each other, lining up the place values.

```
  110
-  50
```

Step 2

Subtract the ones.

```
  110
-  50
    0
```

Step 3

Move to the tens.

You cannot take 5 tens away from 1 ten. Regroup the 1 hundred into 10 tens.

Cross out the 1 hundred to show that there are no hundreds.

Cross out the 1 ten. Show that you added the 10 tens to the 1 ten by writing 11 above the tens place.

```
  0 11
  1̶1̶0
 − 50
    0
```

Step 4

Subtract the tens.

```
  0 11
  1̶1̶0
 − 50
   60
```

The answer is 110 – 50 = 60.

Use the following information to answer the next question.

To get to the next city, a circus travelled 135 kilometres on the first day and 430 kilometres on the second day.

19. How far did the circus travel in total?
    A. 430 km
    B. 530 km
    C. 535 km
    D. 565 km

Use the following information to answer the next question.

These two groups of base ten blocks show a subtraction problem.

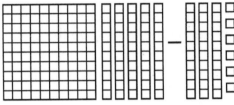

20. When the subtraction problem is solved, what is the difference?
    A. 114
    B. 122
    C. 124
    D. 194

3N1.10 Apply mental mathematics strategies and number properties.

USING MENTAL STRATEGIES TO LEARN BASIC FACTS

A **mental strategy** is a plan that can help you add or subtract quickly in your head.

These are some examples of mental strategies that may help you.

USING DOUBLES

To make facts easier to solve, you can use the strategy of doubles. Change one of the numbers so that the two numbers in the expression are the same. Then, add or subtract the extra digit.

Here are some examples:

- To add 5 + 7, think of 6 + 6 or 5 + 5 + 2.
- To add 8 + 9, think of 8 + 8 + 1 or 9 + 9 – 1.

Example
    Use doubles to add 7 + 8 in your head.

Solution
    Method 1
    Make a double of the first number.
    Think of 7 + 8 as 7 + 7 + 1.
    7 + 7 + 1 = 15

Method 2

Make a double of the second number.

Think of 7 + 8 as 8 + 8 – 1.

8 + 8 – 1 = 15

The answer is 7 + 8 = 15.

MAKING A TEN

To make a fact easier to solve, you can make a ten. This means you make one of the numbers equal to 10. Then, add the rest of the number.

Example

Use the strategy of making a ten to add 9 + 6 in your head.

Solution

When you use the strategy of making a ten, look for the number that is closest to a multiple of 10. You can change this number to be a multiple of 10.

In 9 + 6, the 9 is closest to a multiple of 10. To change 9 into 10, you need to add 1.

Then, take 1 away from the 6 so the 6 will become a 5.

9 + 6 = ?

10 + 5 = 15

USING ADDITION FOR SUBTRACTION

Addition and subtraction are opposite operations. For example, the addition fact 2 + 3 = 5 is the opposite of the subtraction fact 5 – 3 = 2. Both facts use the same three numbers.

To solve a harder subtraction fact, think of the related addition fact.

Example

Use addition to subtract 17 – 9 in your head.

Solution

Think of the number that needs to be added to 9 to make 17.

If you know that 9 + 8 = 17, then you know that 17 – 9 = 8.

REORDERING NUMBERS

You can add numbers in any order, and the answer will still be the same. For example, 5 + 7 = 12 and 7 + 5 = 12.

Example

Reorder the numbers to help you add 6 + 9 in your head.

Solution

If 6 + 9 seems to be a difficult fact, think of 9 + 6.

If you know 9 + 6 = 15, then you know that 6 + 9 = 15.

USING THE ZERO RULE

When zero is added to any number, the answer will always be that number. For example, 11 + 0 = 11.

When zero is subtracted from any number, the answer will always be that number. For example, 10 – 0 = 10.

Example

Use the zero rule to subtract 17 – 0 in your head.

Solution

Since zero is being subtracted, the number 17 will not change.
17 – 0 = 17

21. Ben used doubles to add 9 + 7 in his head. Which of the following strategies shows how Ben added 9 + 7?

A. 9 + 9 + 2

B. 7 + 7 + 2

C. 9 + 1 + 6

D. 7 + 3 + 6

Use the following information to answer the next question.

Cara used the strategy of making a ten to add 8 + 6 in her head.

22. Which of the following strategies shows how Cara added 8 + 6?

A. 6 + 6 + 2

B. 8 + 8 – 2

C. 8 + 3 + 3

D. 6 + 4 + 4

3N1.11 Demonstrate an understanding of multiplication to 5 × 5.

UNDERSTANDING MULTIPLICATION

There are many different ways to explain multiplication.

EQUAL GROUPING

Multiplication can be explained as equal grouping. This means that there are the same number of items in each group.

Example

Show 2 × 5 by making equal groups.

Solution

To show 2 × 5, make 2 groups with 5 items in each group. There will be a total of 10 items.

The equal groupings could look like this.

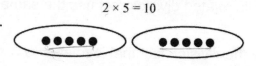

ARRAYS

Multiplication can be explained by making an array. An array shows items placed in equal rows and equal columns. The rows and columns make a rectangular shape.

Example

Draw an array to show 3 × 3.

Solution

To show 3 × 3, make three rows with three items in each row.

The array you draw could look like this.

REPEATED ADDITION

Multiplication can be explained as **repeated addition**. This means that you add the same number to itself over and over.

One number of the fact tells you what number to add over and over. The other number tells you how many times to add that number.

Copyright Protected

Example

Write 4 × 3 by using repeated addition.

Solution

To write 4 × 3 as repeated addition, add 3 to itself four times.
3 + 3 + 3 + 3 = 12
4 × 3 = 12

Another way to write 4 × 3 as repeated addition is to add 4 to itself three times.
4 + 4 + 4 = 12
4 × 3 = 12

RELATING MULTIPLICATION TO DIVISION

Multiplication can be explained as the opposite of division. This means that a multiplication fact and its related division fact use the same three numbers.

Example

Write the division fact that is related to 3 × 8 = 24.

Solution

The related division fact uses the same three numbers.

Start with the total number (24), and divide by either of the other two numbers (8 or 3).
24 ÷ 8 = 3 or 24 ÷ 3 = 8

Use the following information to answer the next question.

Janet needs to solve the problem 3 × 2 = □.

23. Which of the following repeated addition sentences can Janet use to solve the problem?

A. 2 + 2 = □

B. 3 + 2 = □

C. 2 + 2 + 2 = □

D. 3 + 3 + 3 = □

24. Which of the following arrays shows the multiplication sentence 2 × 7 = 14?

A.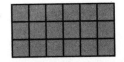

B.

C.

D.

3N1.12 Demonstrate an understanding of division.

UNDERSTANDING DIVISION

There are many different ways to explain division.

EQUAL SHARING

Division can be explained as equal sharing. Equal sharing is the number of items each group will have when a given number of items are shared.

Example

Six candies are shared equally by three students.

Use equal sharing to find how many candies each student will get.

Solution

To show 6 ÷ 3, make 3 groups. Place one candy in each group until all 6 candies are shared.

The groups you make can look like this.
6 ÷ 3 = 2

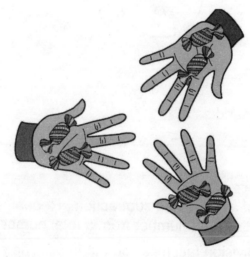

Each student will get 2 candies.

EQUAL GROUPING

Division can be explained as equal grouping. Equal grouping is the number of equal groups you can make out of a total number of items.

Example

Jordan has 6 candies. He gives 2 candies each to some of his friends.

Show 6 ÷ 2 as equal groups to find how many friends will get candy.

Solution

To show 6 ÷ 2, place two candies in each group until all 6 candies are used.

The equal groups you make can look like this.

6 ÷ 2 = 3
Three friends will get candies.

REPEATED SUBTRACTION

Division can be explained as **repeated subtraction**. Repeated subtraction is the number of times you can subtract a given number from a total number.

The larger number of a division fact tells you the total. The smaller number tells you the number to subtract over and over until you reach zero.

Example

Write 12 ÷ 4 as repeated subtraction.

Solution

Start with 12, and subtract 4 over and over until you reach zero. The answer to 12 ÷ 4 is the number of times you subtract 4.

12 − 4 = 8
8 − 4 = 4
4 − 4 = 0

You subtracted 4 three times, so 12 ÷ 4 = 3.

The repeated subtraction that explains 12 ÷ 4 is 12 − 4 − 4 − 4.

Example

    Write the division fact that is shown by the repeated subtraction 9 – 3 – 3 – 3.

Solution

    The larger number that starts the repeated subtraction is the total number. Write 9 followed by a division sign.
$9 \div$

    The number that is repeatedly being subtracted is what 9 is being divided by. Write 3 to the right of the division sign.
$9 \div 3$

    The number of times 3 is subtracted is the answer to $9 \div 3$.

    Since 3 was subtracted three times, $9 \div 3 = 3$.

RELATING DIVISION TO MULTIPLICATION

The same array can be used to show division facts and their related multiplication facts. The related facts all use the same three numbers.

Example

    Arthur makes an array out of these cookies.

    Write two division facts and two multiplication facts for the given array.

Solution

Step 1
Figure out what the array is showing.

- There are 24 cookies in all.
- There are 4 groups of cookies.
- There are 6 cookies in each group.

Step 2
Write two related division facts.
$24 \div 6 = 4$
$24 \div 4 = 6$

Step 3
Write two related multiplication facts.
$4 \times 6 = 24$
$6 \times 4 = 24$

---

25. Which of the following arrays represents 25 ÷ 5?

A.

B.

C.

D.

26. The multiplication fact that is related to 20 ÷ 4 = 5 is

   A. 4 × 4 = 16

   B. 5 × 5 = 25

   C. 4 × 5 = 20

   D. 2 × 10 = 20

3N1.13 Demonstrate an understanding of fractions.

FRACTIONS

A fraction has two parts: a numerator and a denominator. A line separates the two parts.

The numerator is the top number. It shows the number of equal shaded or non-shaded parts. The denominator is the bottom number. It shows the total number of equal parts.

USING A FRACTION TO SHOW A PART OF A WHOLE

A fraction can be written to show equal parts of a whole. For example, the fraction $\frac{3}{4}$ shows that 3 of the 4 parts are not shaded on this fraction strip.

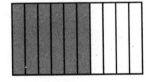

$\frac{3}{4}$ — numerator / denominator

Example

What fraction does the shaded part show?

Solution

Step 1
Count the number of shaded sections. There are six sections shaded. This number (6) is the numerator.

Step 2

Count the total number of sections in the whole. There are 10 sections altogether. This number (10) is the denominator. The denominator is the total number of pieces the whole is divided into.

Write the fraction with the numerator (6) on top of the line and the denominator (10) below the line.

The shaded part of the figure shows the fraction $\frac{6}{10}$.

USING A PICTURE TO SHOW A FRACTION

To show a fraction with a picture, be sure to divide the fraction wheel or fraction strip into equal parts. The denominator tells you the total number of parts. Then, shade the correct number of parts. The numerator tells you the number of parts to shade.

Example

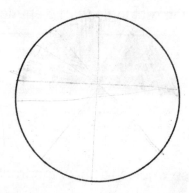

Use this circle to show the fraction $\frac{4}{8}$.

Solution

Step 1

Divide the circle into equal parts.

Since the denominator is 8, divide the circle into 8 equal parts.

Step 2
Shade in any four parts.
Since the numerator is 4, shade in any four parts. The four do not need to be side by side.

COMPARING FRACTIONS WITH LIKE DENOMINATORS

When two or more fractions have the same denominators, compare the numerators to figure out which fraction is greater. For example, the fraction $\frac{2}{3}$ is greater than $\frac{1}{3}$ because 2 shaded parts cover more of the rectangle than 1 shaded part.

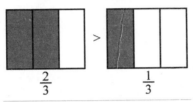

Example

Travis shades parts of these wholes to show the fractions $\frac{3}{4}$ and $\frac{1}{4}$.

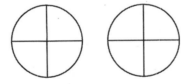

Explain which fraction is greater.

Solution

Step 1
Shade the wholes.

To show $\frac{3}{4}$, Travis could shade any 3 parts.

To show $\frac{1}{4}$, Travis could shade any 1 part.

Step 2
Compare the fractions.

The fraction $\frac{3}{4}$ is greater than $\frac{1}{4}$ because 3 shaded parts cover more of the circle than 1 shaded part.

The numerator 3 is greater than the numerator 2.

Use the following information to answer the next question.

Some fraction strips are shown.

Written Response

27. Using one of these fraction strips, show the fraction $\frac{3}{8}$.

28. Which of the following fractions is greater than $\frac{3}{6}$ but less than $\frac{5}{6}$?

A. $\frac{1}{6}$

B. $\frac{6}{6}$

C. $\frac{4}{6}$

D. $\frac{2}{6}$

Use the following information to answer the next question.

Carlos makes this fraction circle. He shades a part of the circle in.

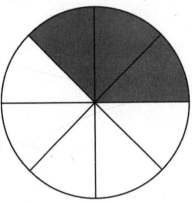

29. What fraction of the circle is **not shaded**?

A. $\frac{3}{5}$

B. $\frac{3}{8}$

C. $\frac{5}{3}$

D. $\frac{5}{8}$

ANSWERS AND SOLUTIONS

NUMBER

1.	C	7.	WR	13.	D	19.	D	25.	C
2.	D	8.	C	14.	C	20.	A	26.	C
3.	D	9.	WR	15.	D	21.	B	27.	WR
4.	B	10.	D	16.	C	22.	D	28.	C
5.	WR	11.	D	17.	A	23.	C	29.	D
6.	WR	12.	D	18.	D	24.	D		

1. C

Step 1

Examine each option.

- Count back by 2s: The numbers will all end in 9, 7, 5, 3, or 1 (odd numbers). The seventh count from 791 is 777.
- Count back by 5s: The numbers will all end in a 6 or 1. The seventh count from 791 is 756.
- Count back by 10s: The numbers will all end in 1. The seventh count from 791 is 721.
- Count back by 100s: The numbers will all end in 91. The seventh count from 791 is 91.

Step 2

Identify the correct option.

The seven counts made from 791 were 781, 771, 761, 751, 741, 731, and 721.

Megan was skip counting backward by 10.

2. D

Step 1

Count the 33 pennies by 1s.

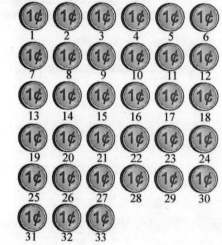

The value of 33 pennies is 33¢, or $0.33.

Step 2

Count the 22 nickels by 5s.

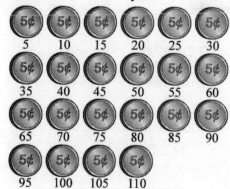

The value of 22 nickels is $1.10.

Step 3
Count the 15 dimes by 10s.

10 20 30 40 50

60 70 80 90 100

110 120 130 140 150

The value of 15 dimes is $1.50.

Step 4
Count the 11 quarters by 25s.

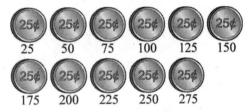

25 50 75 100 125 150

175 200 225 250 275

The value of 11 quarters is $2.75.

Step 5
Determine the greatest value.

Order the amounts of money from least to greatest.
$0.33, $1.10, $1.50, $2.75

The pile of coins that has the greatest value is the pile with 11 quarters ($2.75).

3. D

Step 1
Find the value of each set of blocks.

- 1 hundred flat →100
- 10 ten rods →100
- 8 units →8

Step 2
Add the numbers together.
100 + 100 + 8 = 208

The base ten blocks show the number 208.

4. B

The multiple of 100 that comes before 600 is 500.

In written words, the multiple of 100 that comes before 600 is five hundred.

5. WR

Step 1
Determine the place value of each digit in the number 437.

H	T	O
4	3	7

Step 2

Show the value of each digit with base ten blocks.

To show 4 hundreds, use 4 hundred flats.

To show 3 tens, use 3 ten rods.

To show 7 ones, use 7 units.

Using the fewest base ten blocks, the number 437 can be built with four hundred flats, three ten rods, and seven units.

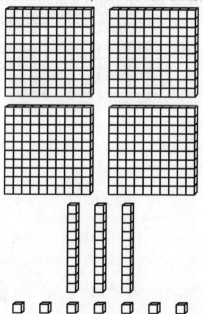

6. WR

Step 1

Compare the hundreds.

Since all three numbers have 5 hundreds, compare the digits in the tens place.

Step 2

Compare the tens.

565, 595, 580

Since 6 is less than 8 and 8 is less than 9, the order of the numbers is 565, 580, and 595.

This number line shows the order of the numbers.

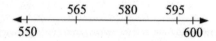

7. WR

Step 1

Write the numbers below each other, lining up the place values.

818
955
839

Step 2

Compare the hundreds.

818
955
839

Since 9 is greater than 8, the number with the greatest value is 955.

Step 3

Compare the tens for 818 and 839.

818
839

Since 1 is less than 3, the number 818 is less than 839.

From greatest to least, the numbers are 955, 839, and 818.

8. C

Step 1

Count the number of hundreds in 736.

100, 200, 300, 400, 500, 600, 700

Count to the next hundred.

…400, 500, 600, 700, 800

Step 2
Figure out which hundred is closer to 736.
The number 736 is between 700 and 800.
It is closer to 700.
700, 710, 720, **730**, 740, 750, 760, 770,
780, 790, **800**
In pennies, the number 700 is equal
to $7.00.
The best estimate of 736 pennies is $7.00.

9. **WR**

Step 1
Count the number of stars in one row.
There are 12 stars in a row. Since you do
not need an exact answer when you
estimate, use the number 10 instead of 12
because it is easier to count by 10s
than by 12s.

Step 2
Estimate the number of stars.
Count by 10s as you move from row to row.
Since there are 11 rows, count by 10s a
total of 11 times.
10, 20, 30, 40, 50, 60, 70, 80, 90, 100, 110
There are about 110 stars in the design.

10. **D**

Step 1
Write the hundreds digit.
There are 3 hundred flats. They have a
value of 300. Write the digit 3.
3_ _

Step 2
Write the tens digit.
There are 5 ten rods. They have a value of
50. Write 5 to the right of the 3 to act as a
placeholder.
35_

Step 3
Write the ones digit.
There are no units. Write 0 to the right of 5
as a placeholder.
350
The number shown by the base ten blocks
is 350.

11. **D**

Step 1
Find the value of each digit in the number
153.
The digit 1 has a value of 100.
The digit 5 has a value of 50.
The digit 3 has a value of 3.

Step 2
Figure out which base ten blocks show
the values.
The value of 100 can be shown with one
hundred flat.

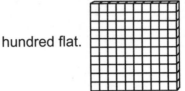

The value of 50 can be shown with five
ten rods.

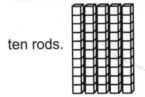

The value of 3 can be shown with
three units.

The values of each digit in the number 153
can be shown with these base ten
blocks.

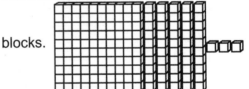

12. **D**

Step 1
Figure out the place value of each digit.

- The first digit 2 has a value of 200.
- The digit 5 has a value of 50.
- The last digit 2 has a value of 2.

None of the choices show the fewest
number of coins.

Step 2

Figure out another way to show the place values.

The number 252 can also be shown with 2 loonies, 4 dimes, and 12 pennies.

13. D

A quick way to add 41 + 56 is to add from left to right.

Step 1
For each number, break them into tens and ones.

Think of 41 as 40 + 1 and 56 as 50 + 6.

Step 2
Add the tens of both numbers together, and add the ones of both numbers together.

Add the tens.
40 + 50 = 90

Add the ones.
1 + 6 = 7

Step 3
Add the tens and ones together.
90 + 7 = 97
The answer is 41 + 56 = 97.

A quick way of adding 41 + 56 is adding the sum of 40 + 50 to the sum of 1 + 6.

14. C

A quick way to add 19 + 15 is to make a zero.

Step 1
Start with the number that is closest to a multiple of 10, and make that number end in zero.

Think of 19 as 20 (19 + 1 = 20).

Step 2
Add the two numbers.
20 + 15 = 35

Step 3

Perform the operation used in step 1 again on the answer you find.
Since you added 1 to 19, subtract 1 from 35.

35 – 1 = 34
20 + 15 – 1 = 34
So, 19 + 15 = 34.

15. D

You could use the mental strategy of making a zero.

Step 1
Change the number being subtracted into the nearest multiple of 10.
Think of 22 as 20 (22 – 2 = 20).

Step 2
Subtract the two numbers.
46 – 20 = 26

Step 3
Perform the operation used in step 1 again on the answer you find.
Since you subtracted 2 from 20, subtract 2 from 26.
26 – 2 = 24

16. C

Step 1
Starting with the number being subtracted, add on numbers that are easy to work with as you count up to the greater number.

- First, think 38 + $\boxed{2}$ = 40.

- Next, think 40 + $\boxed{10}$ = 50.

- Then, think 50 + $\boxed{1}$ = 51.

Step 2
Find the sum of the numbers you added on.
2 + 10 + 1 = 13

The sum will be the answer to the subtraction problem. This means the answer is 51 – 38 = 13.
The equations 38 + 2 = 40, 40 + 10 = 50, and 50 + 1 = 51 show Jesse's strategy of adding on.

17. A

Step 1
Keep the first digit of each number, and change the last digit of each number to zero.
44 →40
17 →10
To estimate the difference of 44 – 17, use 40 – 10.

Step 2
Subtract the two numbers.
40 – 10 = 30
Dani has about 30 hair clips left.

18. D

Step 1
Use front-end estimation.
Keep the front digits, and replace all the numbers to the right with zeros.
45 → 40
23 → 20

Step 2
Add the two numbers.
40 + 20 = 60
To estimate the sum of 45 + 23, Zack used 40 + 20 = 60.

19. D

Choice D is correct. The circus travelled 565 kilometres in total in two days.

To find out how far the circus travelled in two days, add the two distances.

135 km (first day)
+430 km (second day)
565 km

20. A

Step 1
Find the value of each group of base ten blocks.
The value of the first group is 100 (1 flat) plus 50 (5 ten rods).
100
+50
150
The value of the second group is 30 (3 ten rods) plus 6 (6 units).
30
+6
36

Step 2
Subtract the two numbers to find the difference.

  4 10
15?0?
– 36
114
The difference is 114.

21. B

There are two ways to use doubles.

Think of 9 + 7 as 7 + 7 + 2.
7 + 7 + 2 = 16

Think of 9 + 7 as 9 + 9 – 2.
9 + 9 – 2 = 16

The answer is 9 + 7 = 16.

Of the choices given, Ben used 7 + 7 + 2 to add 9 + 7 in his head.

22. D

There are two ways to make a ten.

Method 1
Think of making 8 into a 10.
Think 8 + 2 + 4.
8 + 2 + 4 = 14
The answer is 8 + 6 = 14.

Method 2

Think of making 6 into a 10.

Think $\boxed{6+4}+4$.

$6 + 4 + 4 = 14$

The answer is $8 + 6 = 14$.

Of the choices given, Cara used $6 + 4 + 4$ to add $8 + 6$ in her head.

23. C

There are two ways to explain 3×2 as repeated addition.

One way is to add 2 to itself three times. $2 + 2 + 2 = 6$

Another way is to add 3 to itself two times. $3 + 3 = 6$

Of the choices given, the repeated addition of $2 + 2 + 2 = \square$ can help Janet solve the problem.

24. D

Step 1

Identify all the multiplication sentences shown by the arrays.

This is a 3 by 6 array, so $3 \times 6 = 18$.

This is a 4 by 3 array, so $4 \times 3 = 12$.

This is a 2 by 8 array, so $2 \times 8 = 16$.

This is a 2 by 7 array, so $2 \times 7 = 14$.

Step 2

Match the multiplication sentence with the correct figure.

This figure shows $2 \times 7 = 14$.

25. C

To show $25 \div 5$, there must be a total of 25 squares.

Each row must have 5 squares until all 25 squares are used.

This array shows $25 \div 5$.

There are 5 squares in each of the 5 rows. $25 \div 5 = 5$

26. C

Multiplication and division are opposite or inverse operations.

This means that you can use the numbers in a division fact to create two related multiplication facts.

The division fact $20 \div 4 = 5$ is related to the multiplication facts $4 \times 5 = 20$ and $5 \times 4 = 20$.

27. WR

Step 1

Choose the correct fraction strip.

Since the denominator is 8, choose the strip that has 8 equal parts.

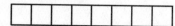

Step 2

Figure out how many parts to shade.

Since the numerator is 3, shade any 3 parts.

This fraction strip shows the fraction $\frac{3}{8}$.

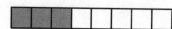

28. C

Fractions that have the same denominators (the bottom value) can be compared by looking at the numerators (the top value).

A fraction greater than $\frac{3}{6}$ would have a 4, 5, or 6 in the numerator. Since you are looking for the fraction that is also less than $\frac{5}{6}$, only 4 is in between 3 and 5.

The fraction greater than $\frac{3}{6}$ but less than $\frac{5}{6}$ is $\frac{4}{6}$.

29. D

Step 1
Figure out the numerator.
There are 5 non-shaded parts. The number 5 becomes the numerator of the fraction.

Step 2
Figure out the denominator.
The circle has a total of eight parts.
The number 8 becomes the denominator of the fraction.
The fraction of the circle that is not shaded is $\frac{5}{8}$.

Unit Test — Number

Use the following information to answer the next question.

Lily starts at the number 350 and counts up by 25s.

1. What number will Lily reach after seven counts?
   A. 175
   B. 525
   C. 550
   D. 700

Use the following information to answer the next question.

Don counts backward by 100.
700, 600, 500

2. Written in words, the next number is
   A. six hundred
   B. four hundred
   C. forty hundred
   D. five hundred one

Use the following information to answer the next question.

Jay sees these base ten blocks on the table at the back of the math room.

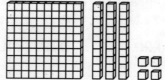

3. What number do the base ten blocks show?
   A. 134
   B. 143
   C. 413
   D. 431

Written Response

4. Build the number 296 using the smallest number of base ten blocks.

Use the following information to answer the next question.

A set of numbers is given.
121, 90, 714, 264, 710

5. Listed in order from least to greatest, the numbers are
   A. 90, 121, 264, 710, and 714
   B. 714, 710, 264, 121, and 90
   C. 710, 714, 121, 264, and 90
   D. 90, 710, 264, 121, and 714

Use the following information to answer the next question.

A jar is filled with 672 candies.

6. Using 100 as a referent, about how many candies are in the jar?
   A. 600
   B. 650
   C. 670
   D. 700

7. Which of the following sets of base ten blocks shows the value of each digit in the number 303?

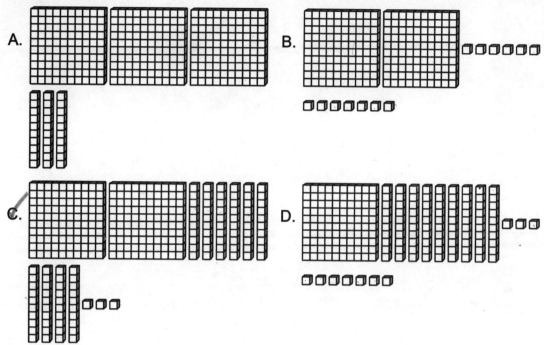

8. Which of the following groups of coins shows the value of the first digit of the number 555?

A.

B.

C.

D.

9. Laura used the strategy of doubles to subtract 96 – 48 in her head. Which of the following strategies did she use?

A. 96 – 50 and 46 + 2

B. 48 + 48 and 96 – 48

C. 48 + 2, 50 + 46, and 2 + 46

D. 40 + 40, 90 + 4, and 100 – 16

10. Which of the following mental strategies could be used to quickly subtract 70 – 22 in your head?

A. 70 – 2 = 68, then 68 + 2 = □

B. 70 – 2 = 68, then 68 – 2 = □

C. 70 – 20 = 50, then 50 – 2 = □

D. 70 – 20 = 50, then 50 + 2 = □

Use the following information to answer the next question.

Paul has 85 coloured pencils. Of the 85 pencils, 16 are red. He uses front-end estimation to figure out about how many pencils are not red.

11. Which estimate does Paul use?

A. 90 – 20

B. 90 – 10

C. 80 – 20

D. 80 – 10

Use the following information to answer the next question.

One lap around the school's race track is 420 metres. Peter has run 250 metres.

12. How many more metres does Peter need to run to finish one lap?
    A. 170 m   B. 180 m
    C. 230 m   D. 270 m

Use the following information to answer the next question.

Students are decorating gingerbread cookies for a bake sale. There are 176 boys at the school, and there are 31 more girls than boys at the school.

13. How many gingerbread cookies are needed so that each student can decorate one cookie?
    A. 145   B. 207
    C. 321   D. 383

Use the following information to answer the next question.

Mark used an addition strategy to subtract 16 – 7 in his head.

14. Which of the following strategies shows how Mark subtracted 16 – 7?
    A. 16 – 6 + 1   B. 16 – 2 – 7
    C. 7 + 9   D. 8 + 7

15. Which of the following diagrams represents 2 × 6?
    A.    B.

    C. ♥♥♥♥♥♥ ♥♥♥♥♥♥   D.

16. The division fact 20 ÷ 5 can be explained as the repeated subtraction
    A. 20 – 10 – 10   B. 20 – 5 – 5 – 5
    C. 20 – 5 – 5 – 5 – 5   D. 20 – 4 – 4 – 4 – 4 – 4

17. Which of the following figures represents the fraction $\frac{3}{4}$?
    A.   B.
    C.   D.

18. Which of the following sets of fractions are ordered from least to greatest?

A. $\frac{3}{5}, \frac{2}{5}, \frac{4}{5}$

B. $\frac{3}{4}, \frac{2}{4}, \frac{1}{4}$

C. $\frac{1}{3}, \frac{3}{3}, \frac{2}{3}$

D. $\frac{1}{5}, \frac{2}{5}, \frac{5}{5}$

ANSWERS AND SOLUTIONS — UNIT TEST

1. B	6. D	11. D	16. C
2. B	7. C	12. A	17. C
3. A	8. D	13. D	18. D
4. WR	9. B	14. C	
5. A	10. C	15. C	

1. B

Start with 350, and add 25 to each number to get the next number. Do this for seven counts.

350, 375, 400, 425, 450, 475, 500, 525

Lily will reach the number 525 after seven counts.

2. B

Step 1

Figure out the next number.

The next number is 100 less than 500.

500 – 100 = 400

Step 2

Write in words.

Written in words, 400 is four hundred.

3. A

Step 1

Determine the number of hundreds, tens, and ones.

The base ten blocks are made up of 1 hundred flat (100), 3 ten rods (30), and 4 units (4).

Step 2

Add the numbers together.

100 + 30 + 4 = 134

The base ten blocks show the number 134.

4. WR

Step 1

Find the number of hundreds, tens, and ones in the number.

In 296, there are 2 hundreds, 9 tens, and 6 ones.

Step 2

Show the place values using base ten blocks.

To show 2 hundreds, use 2

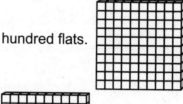

hundred flats.

To show 9 tens, use 9 ten rods.

To show 6 ones, use 6 units.

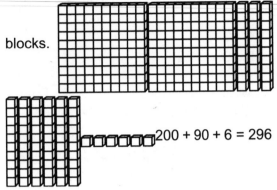

Step 3

Put the blocks together.

Using the fewest base ten blocks, the number 296 is shown with these

blocks.

$200 + 90 + 6 = 296$

5. A

Step 1

Separate any two-digit numbers from the three-digit numbers.

The only two-digit number is 90. It is lower in value than any of the three-digit numbers.

Step 2

Write the three-digit numbers below each other, lining up the place values.

121
714
264
710

Step 3

Compare the hundreds.

121
714
264
710

Since 1 is less than 2, 121 is less than 264.

Step 4

Compare the tens of 714 and 710.

714
710

Since both numbers have one ten, compare the ones.

Step 5

Compare the ones.

Since 0 is less than 1, 710 is less than 714.

From least to greatest, the numbers are 90, 121, 264, 710, and 714.

6. D

Step 1

Count the number of hundreds in 672.
100, 200, 300, 400, 500, 600
Count to the next hundred.
100, 200, 300, 400, 500, 600, 700
The number 672 is between 600 and 700.

Step 2

Figure out which hundred is closer to 672.
Count by 10s.
600, 610, 620, 630, 640, 650, 660, **670**,
680, 690, **700**
The number 672 is closer to 700.
There are about 700 candies in the jar.

7. C

Step 1

Figure out the place value of each digit.
The first digit 3 has a value of 300.
The 0 has no value. It shows that there are no tens.
The second 3 has a value of 3.

Step 2

Use base ten blocks to represent the number.

The number 303 could be shown like this, but none of the choices show the fewest number of base ten blocks.

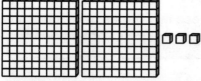

Show the place values another way.

The number 303 can also be shown with 2 hundred flats, 10 ten rods, and 3 units.

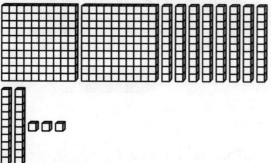

8. D

Step 1

Determine the first digit.

In a three-digit number, the first digit is the digit on the left.

555

Step 2

Determine the value of the first 5.

The first 5 has a value of 500.

It is shown with 5 dollar coins.

Each $1 coin represents 100 ¢.

100 + 100 + 100 + 100 + 100 = 500 ¢

9. B

Think of the smaller number (48) as a double.

Since 48 + 48 = 96, then 96 − 48 = 48.

10. C

A quick way to subtract 70 − 22 is to make a zero.

Step 1

Change the number being subtracted into the nearest multiple of 10.

Think of 22 as 20 (22 − 2 = 20).

Step 2

Subtract the two numbers.

Subtract 20 from 70.

70 − 20 = 50

Step 3

Perform the operation used in step 1 again on the answer you find.

Since you subtracted 2 from 22, subtract 2 from 50.

50 − 2 = 48

The mental strategy that could be used to quickly subtract 70 − 22 is 70 − 20 = 50 and then 50 − 2 = □.

11. D

Step 1

For both numbers, keep the first digit, and replace the last digit with a zero.

85 → 80

16 → 10

To estimate the difference of 85 − 16, use 80 − 10.

Step 2

Subtract the two numbers.

80 − 10 = 70

The estimate Paul used is 80 − 10.

12. A

Choice A mA

To solve this problem, subtract the two numbers. 420 − 250

$$\begin{array}{r} \overset{3\ 12}{4\cancel{2}0} \\ -250 \\ \hline 170 \end{array}$$

13. D

Step 1

Figure out the number of girls.

There are 176 boys at the school.

Since there are 31 more girls than boys, add 176 and 31 to find the number of girls.

$$\begin{array}{r}\overset{1}{1}76\\+31\\\hline207\end{array}$$

There are 207 girls in the school.

Step 2

Figure out the total number of students.

Add the number of girls (207) and the number of boys (176).

$$\begin{array}{r}\overset{1}{}207\\+176\\\hline383\end{array}$$

There are 383 students at the school. D383 gingerbreadD

14. C

Think of the number that needs to be added to 7 to make 16.

If you know that 7 + 9 = 16 (or 9 + 7 = 16), then you know that 16 − 7 = 9.

The strategy Mark used was 7 + 9.

15. C

Multiplication can be shown as equal grouping.

The multiplication fact 2 × 6 can be shown as 2 equal groups of 6.

This diagram shows 2 equal groups with 6 hearts in each group.

16. C

Start with 20, and subtract 5 over and over until you reach zero. The answer to 20 ÷ 5 is the number of times you subtract 5.

20 − 5 = 15
15 − 5 = 10
10 − 5 = 5
  5 − 5 = 0

You subtracted 5 four times, so 20 ÷ 5 = 4.

The repeated subtraction that explains 20 ÷ 5 is 20 − 5 − 5 − 5 − 5.

17. C

Step 1

Identify the figures that show the denominator.

Since the denominator of the fraction is 4, the figures must have four equal parts.

Only these two figures have four parts.

Step 2

Identify the figure that shows the numerator.

Since the numerator is 3, the figure must have three shaded parts.

This figure represents the fraction $\frac{3}{4}$.

18. D

This set of fractions $\frac{1}{5}, \frac{2}{5}, \frac{5}{5}$, is ordered from least to greatest.

Since the denominators are the same, compare the numerators. The smaller the numerator, the smaller the fraction.

The number 1 is less than 2, and 2 is less than 5 or 1 < 2, and 2 < 5.

Patterns and Relations

PATTERNS AND RELATIONS

Table of Correlations			
Outcome	Practice Questions	Unit Test Questions	Practice Test
3PR1.0 Use patterns to describe the world and to solve problems.			
3PR1.1 Demonstrate an understanding of increasing patterns, using manipulatives, diagrams, sounds and actions.	1, 2	1, 2	17
3PR1.2 Demonstrate an understanding of decreasing patterns, using manipulatives, diagrams, sounds and actions.	3, 4	3	18
3PR1.3 Sort objects or numbers, using one or more than one attribute.	5, 6, 7	4	19
3PR2.0 Represent algebraic expressions in multiple ways.			
3PR2.4 Solve one-step addition and subtraction equations involving a symbol to represent an unknown number.	8, 9	5	20

3PR1.1 Demonstrate an understanding of increasing patterns, using manipulatives, diagrams, sounds and actions.

INCREASING PATTERNS

An **increasing pattern** is a sequence that gets bigger. Numbers or objects increase in value with each term of the sequence. An increasing pattern is also called a growing pattern. For example, 5, 10, 15, 20 is a growing pattern that increases by 5 each time.

PATTERN RULES

A **pattern rule** can be used to create a pattern. It tells you what number to start the pattern with, what operation to use, and the number or numbers to use with the operation to get the next term. Pattern rules help you to extend or continue a pattern.

In order to make a prediction about which number or shape should appear next in the pattern, you first need to find the pattern rule being used. Then, continue using the rule to make the prediction.

Example

Peter built these shapes with coloured links.

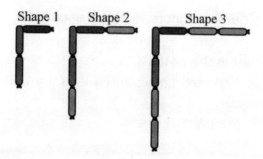

According to the pattern rule Peter used, how many links will be in shape 4?

Solution

Step 1

Count the number of links in each shape to determine the pattern rule.

- In shape 1, there are three links.
- In shape 2, there are five links.
- In shape 3, there are seven links.

The pattern rule is to add two links to each shape to make the next shape.

Step 2

Apply the pattern rule to find the number of links in shape 4.

7 + 2 = 9

There will be nine links in shape 4.

Example

This pattern of numbers has one number missing.

44, 48, 52, _____, 60, 64

What is the missing number in the pattern?

Solution

Step 1

Determine the pattern.

The given sequence is 44, 48, 52,?, 60, and 64.

Count up from one number to the next number.

- Starting at 44, count 45, 46, 47, 48. That is 4 counts.
- Starting at 48, count 49, 50, 51, 52. That is 4 counts again.

The pattern is that the numbers increase by 4 each time.

You can also find the pattern by adding.

- The first number is 44.
- The second number is 44 + 4 = 48.
- The third number is 48 + 4 = 52.

The pattern is that the numbers increase by 4 each time.

Step 2

Find the missing number in the pattern.

The missing number is 4 more than 52 and 4 less than 60.

52 + 4 = 56 or 60 − 4 = 56

The missing number in the pattern is 56.

Use the following information to answer the next question.

Mr. Scott writes the following number pattern on the board:

67, 77, 87, 97, _____, _____

1. In order, which two numbers belong in the blanks?

    A. 97 and 107

    B. 107 and 117

    C. 107 and 127

    D. 117 and 127

Use the following information to answer the next question.

Eva used a pattern to make these three figures out of marbles.

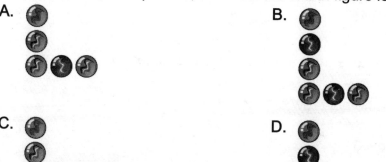

2. If Eva continues the pattern, what will the fourth figure look like?

A.

B.

C.

D.

3PR1.2 Demonstrate an understanding of decreasing patterns, using manipulatives, diagrams, sounds and actions.

DECREASING PATTERNS

A **decreasing pattern** is a sequence that gets smaller. Numbers and objects decrease with each term of the sequence. A decreasing pattern is also called a shrinking pattern. For example, 17, 15, 13, 11 is a shrinking pattern that decreases by 2 each time.

PATTERN RULES

A **pattern rule** can be used to create a pattern. It tells you what number to start the pattern with, what operation to use, and what to do to get the next term. Pattern rules help you extend or continue a pattern.

In order to make a prediction about which number or shape should appear next in the pattern, you first need to find the pattern rule being used. Then, continue using the rule to make the prediction.

Example

The teacher gave her class this pattern of stars.

Row 1 ☆☆☆☆☆☆☆☆☆☆☆☆☆☆

Row 2 ☆☆☆☆☆☆☆☆☆☆☆☆

Row 3 ☆☆☆☆☆☆☆☆☆☆

Row 4 ☆☆☆☆☆☆☆☆

Row 5 ☆☆☆☆☆☆

Use the pattern rule shown to find out how many stars will be in row 6.

Solution

Step 1

Count the number of stars in each row to determine the pattern rule.

- In row 1, there are 16 stars.
- In row 2, there are 14 stars.
- In row 3, there are 12 stars.
- In row 4, there are 10 stars.
- In row 5, there are 8 stars.

The pattern rule is to subtract 2 from each row of stars to get the next row.

Step 2

Apply the pattern rule for the next row of stars.

$8 - 2 = 6$

There will be 6 stars in row 6.

Example

This series of numbers has one term missing.

48, 44, 40, 36, _____, 28

What is the missing term in the given series? _____

Solution

Step 1

Find the difference between the numbers.

$48 - 44 = 4$

$44 - 40 = 4$

$40 - 36 = 4$

The difference between two consecutive terms is 4.

Step 2

Find the missing number in the pattern.

It is 4 less than 36 and 4 more than 28.

$36 - 4 = 32$ or $28 + 4 = 32$

The missing term in the series is 32.

Use the following information to answer the next question.

Lacey writes the following number pattern: 28, 24, 20, 16

3. Which pattern rule explains Lacey's number pattern?

A. Add 2 each time.

B. Add 4 each time.

C. Subtract 2 each time.

D. Subtract 4 each time.

4. Which number pattern is shrinking by 7 each time?
   A. 14, 21, 28, 35
   B. 56, 49, 41, 32
   C. 63, 56, 49, 42
   D. 92, 84, 76, 68

3PR1.3 Sort objects or numbers, using one or more than one attribute.

SORTING NUMBERS AND OBJECTS

Numbers and objects can be sorted using many different ways.

SORTING NUMBERS

Numbers can be sorted by looking at certain features. Here are some of the features you can use to sort numbers:

- Even or odd
- One or two digits
- Greater than or less than
- Fractions or whole numbers

For example, these two groups of numbers are sorted by the number of digits.

- Group 1: The numbers 1, 2, 3, and 7 are made up of one digit.
- Group 2: The numbers 11, 24, 59, and 67 are made up of two digits.

Numbers are often sorted into groups of either odd and even numbers or greater than and less than numbers. Sometimes, numbers are sorted using both of these characteristics.

Example

Mr. Sommer gave his students this list of numbers and asks them to sort the numbers into different groups.

2, 5, 6, 9, 12, 15, 16, 19, 20, 21, 24, 25

He wants them to sort the numbers according to whether they are less than 13 or 13 and greater and whether they are even or odd.

Sort the numbers into the given chart.

	Even	Odd
< 13		
13 or > 13		

Solution

Step 1

Classify the numbers as even or odd.

If a number can be divided evenly into two equal groups, it is even. The even numbers are 2, 6, 12, 16, 20, and 24.

If a number cannot be divided evenly into two groups, it is odd. The odd numbers are 5, 9, 15, 19, 21, and 25.

Step 2

Classify the even and odd numbers as less than 13 or 13 and greater.

The numbers 2, 6, and 12 are even and less than 13.

The numbers 5 and 9 are odd and less than 13.

The numbers 16, 20, and 24 are even and greater than 13.

The numbers 15, 19, 21, and 25 are odd and greater than 13.

Step 3

Write the numbers in the correct boxes of the chart.

- The numbers that are even and less than 13 go in the top left box.
- The numbers that are odd and less than 13 go in the top right box.
- The numbers that are even and greater than 13 go in the bottom left box.
- The numbers that are odd and greater than 13 go in the bottom right box.

This chart shows the list of numbers sorted correctly and placed in the proper boxes.

	Even	Odd
< 13	2, 6, 12	5, 9
13 or > 13	16, 20, 24	15, 19, 21, 25

SORTING OBJECTS

Sometimes, rules are used to sort objects or numbers into groups or sets. These rules may be about lengths of sides or kinds of shapes.

Example

Kyle uses the sorting rule of four equal side lengths or two equal side lengths to sort these quadrilaterals into two groups.

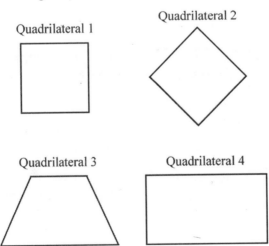

Quadrilateral 1

Quadrilateral 2

Quadrilateral 3

Quadrilateral 4

Which quadrilaterals should Kyle put in each group?

Solution

Step 1

Identify the shapes that have four equal side lengths.

Quadrilateral 1 (the square) and quadrilateral 2 (the rhombus) both have four sides that are the same length. They belong in the first group.

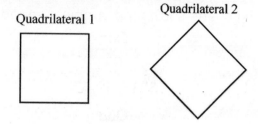

Quadrilateral 1   Quadrilateral 2

Step 2

Identify the shapes that have two equal side lengths.

Quadrilateral 3 (the trapezoid) has one pair of sides that are equal in length. Quadrilateral 4 (the rectangle) each has two pairs of equal side lengths. These two shapes belong in the second group.

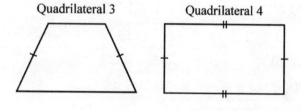

Quadrilateral 3   Quadrilateral 4

Use the following information to answer the next question.

Nadia wants to sort the numbers 72, 69, 19, 4, 30, 25, 3, 18, 56, and 15. She wants to sort them in these ways:

1. Odd or even
2. Greater than 20 or less than 20

---

5. Which of the following charts shows the numbers sorted using the two rules?

A.

	Odd	Even
Greater than 20	69	30, 56, 72
Less than 20	3, 15, 19, 25	4, 18

B.

	Odd	Even
Greater than 20	25, 69	30, 56, 72
Less than 20	3, 15	4, 18, 19

C.

	Odd	Even
Greater than 20	25, 69	30,56, 72
Less than 20	3, 15, 19	4, 18

D.

	Odd	Even
Greater than 20	25, 69, 72	30, 56
Less than 20	3, 15, 19	4, 18

6. Which of the following sets of numbers contains only odd numbers that are greater than 32 but less than 93?

A. 31, 75, 91   B. 51, 89, 95

C. 54, 57, 91   D. 67, 83, 89

Jack has seven pattern blocks.

He sorts the pattern blocks using two rules:
Rule one—angles or no angles
Rule two—black or white

Written Response

7. Sort the pattern blocks using the chart below. Be sure to label the chart using the two sorting rules.

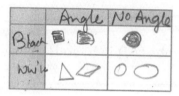

3PR2.4 Solve one-step addition and subtraction equations involving a symbol to represent an unknown number.

SOLVING EQUATIONS

An equation is a number sentence that uses an equal sign (=) to show that both sides have the same value or are balanced. An equal sign tells you "is the same as." A symbol can be used to represent an unknown number in an equation. The symbol can be a letter, a sign, or a shape. A written problem or picture problem can be shown as an equation with an unknown.

A strategy is a plan you can use to help you solve a problem. Pick a strategy that works best for you, and use it to solve problems and equations. Some strategies could be counting up, counting down, using base ten blocks, and using inverse operations.

Example

Bert has a bag with 9 candies in it. He eats 4 of the candies at recess. Bert writes an equation in which *T* represents the number of candies he has left. His equation is $4 + T = 9$.

What is the missing number in Bert's equation?

Solution

One way to solve this problem is to use the strategy of inverse operations. Since the inverse operation of addition is subtraction, use subtraction to find the missing number.

Subtract 4 from 9 to find the value of *T*.

$$4 + T = 9$$
$$T = 9 - 4$$
$$T = 5$$

Bert's equation is now $4 + 5 = 9$.

The value of the missing number (*T*) is 5, so Bert has 5 candies left.

Use the following information to answer the next question.

Jenny knows that 9 of the 16 marbles in her jar are red. To find how many marbles are not red, she writes this equation.

$16 - n = 9$

8. Which of the following numbers is represented by *n* in Jenny's equation?

A. 6   B. 7

C. 8   D. 9

Numerical Response

9. In the equation $13 = \Delta - 3$, what number does Δ represent? _____

ANSWERS AND SOLUTIONS
PATTERNS AND RELATIONS

1. B	4. C	7. WR
2. D	5. C	8. B
3. D	6. D	9. 16

1. B

Choice B is correct. In order, the next two numbers in the number pattern are 107 and 117.

This number pattern counts forward by 10s. The digits in the tens place go up by 1, and the digits in the ones place stay the same (always end in 7).

The first blank in the number pattern will be 10 greater than 97.
97 + 10 = 107

The second blank in the number pattern will be 10 greater than 107.
107 + 10 = 117

2. D

Step 1
Determine the pattern rule.
The pattern starts with 1 marble. Then, 2 marbles are added to the first figure to make the second figure. Then, 2 more marbles are added to the second figure to make the third figure.

- The first figure has 1 marble.
- The second figure has 1 + 2 = 3 marbles.
- The third figure has 3 + 2 = 5 marbles.

The pattern rule is to start with 1 and add 2 for each new figure.

Step 2
Extend the pattern.
To extend the pattern, apply the pattern rule by adding 2 to 5.
The fourth figure has 5 + 2 = 7 marbles.
If Eva continues the pattern, the fourth figure will have seven marbles and will look like this:

3. D

Choice D is correct. The rule that explains the number pattern is subtract 4 each time.
(28 − 4 = 24) (24 − 4 = 20) (20 − 4 = 16)

4. C

Choice C is correct. This number pattern shows a pattern that shrinks by 7 each time.
(63 − 7 = 56) (56 − 7 = 49) (49 − 7 = 42)

The number pattern in choice A counts by 7s, but it is a growing pattern, not a shrinking pattern.

The number pattern in choice B starts shrinking by 7, but then it shrinks by 8 and then by 9.

5. C

Step 1

Sort the numbers as either odd or even.

- The odd numbers will end in a 1, 3, 5, 7, or 9.
  The odd numbers are 69, 19, 25, 3, and 15.
- The even numbers will end in 2, 4, 6, 8, or 0.
  The even numbers are 72, 4, 30, 18, and 56.

Step 2

Sort the odd numbers as greater or less than 20.

- The odd numbers greater than 20 are 69 and 25.
- The odd numbers less than 20 are 19, 3, and 15.

Step 3

Sort the even numbers as greater or less than 20.

- The even numbers greater than 20 are 72, 30, and 56.
- The even numbers less than 20 are 4 and 18.

Step 4

Place the numbers in the correct boxes.

	Odd	Even
Greater than 20	25, 69	30, 56, 72
Less than 20	3, 15, 19	4, 18

6. D

Step 1

Find the range of numbers.

- Since the numbers must be greater than 32, look for numbers that start after 32.
- Since the numbers must also be less than 93, look for numbers that start at 33 and end before 93.

The range of numbers is from 33 to 92.

Step 2

Identify the odd numbers.

Odd numbers are numbers that end in 1, 3, 5, 7, or 9.

Look for numbers that end in 1, 3, 5, 7, or 9 and go from 33 (greater than 32) to 92 (less than 93).

The numbers 67, 83, and 89 are odd numbers that are greater than 32 but less than 93.

7. WR

Correctly sorts all blocks and correctly labels the sorting chart.

	Angles	No Angles
Black	▮ ◗	●
White	◣ ▱	○ ⬭

8. B

Step 1

Use the strategy of related facts.

If $16 - n = 9$, then $16 - 9 = n$.

Step 2

Find the value of n.

If $16 - 9 = 7$, then $n = 7$.

Step 3

Verify the answer.

Substitute the value of 7 for the letter n in the equation.

$16 - n = 9$
$16 - 7 = 9$
$9 = 9$

Since both sides of the equation are the same number or equal, the answer is correct.

9. 16

Step 1

Identify what Δ stands for.

The Δ stands for the number that 3 is subtracted from in order to equal the answer 13.

Switch the two halves of the equation to opposite sides of the equal sign to see the purpose of Δ more clearly.

$Δ - 3 = 13$

Step 2

Use addition to solve the subtraction problem.

If $\triangle - 3 = 13$, then $\triangle = 13 + 3$.

Since $13 + 3 = 16$, $\triangle = 16$.

Copyright Protected

Unit Test — Patterns and Relations

Use the following information to answer the next question.

There are four number patterns shown on the following chart:

Pattern A	1	10	19		
Pattern B	2	10	18		
Pattern C	3	10	17		
Pattern D	4	10	16		

1. In which pattern does the number 31 belong?
   A. Pattern A
   B. Pattern B
   C. Pattern C
   D. Pattern D

Use the following information to answer the next question.

Priti wants to plant some vegetables in her garden plots. She places 4 logs around each vegetable plot.

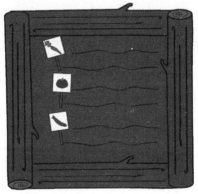

Priti wants to make some more vegetable plots. She starts to make a table.

| Number of vegetable plots | 1 | 2 | 3 | 4 | 5 | 6 | 7 |
| Number of logs | 4 | 8 | 12 | | | | |

2. How many vegetable plots could Priti make with 24 logs?
   A. 4
   B. 5
   C. 6
   D. 7

Unit Test   86   Castle Rock Research

3. Which number pattern shrinks by 5 each time?

    A. 532, 527, 522, 517   B. 535, 540, 545, 550

    C. 555, 545, 535, 525   D. 565, 460, 355, 240

Use the following information to answer the next question.

Justin sorts six shapes using two rules.

- **Rule one**– square or circle
- **Rule two**– black or white

4. Which chart shows the shapes sorted using Justin's two rules?

A.

	Squares	Circles
Black	●■	■
White	○□	○

B.

	Squares	Circles
Black	■	●●
White	□□	○

C.

	Squares	Circles
Black	■■	●
White	□	○○

D.

	Squares	Circles
Black	■	●●
White	□□	○

Numerical Response

5. In the equation $6 + P = 18$, the letter P is equal to _____.

ANSWERS AND SOLUTIONS — UNIT TEST

1. C	3. A	5. 12
2. C	4. C	

1. C

The number 31 belongs in pattern C.

The number 31 cannot belong to patterns B or D because they have all even numbers, and 31 is an odd number.

- Pattern A adds 9 each time:
  $1 + 9 = 10$
  $10 + 9 = 19$
  $19 + 9 = 28$
  $28 + 9 = 37$
  The number 31 does not belong in this pattern.
- Pattern C adds 7 each time:
  $3 + 7 = 10$
  $10 + 7 = 17$
  $17 + 7 = 24$
  $24 + 7 = 31$
  The number 31 belongs in this pattern.

2. C

The number of logs in each vegetable plot is a growing pattern. To find the number of logs, add 4 each time.

- $12 + 4 = 16$
  For 4 plots, she needs 16 logs.
- $16 + 4 = 20$
  For 5 plots, she needs 20 logs.
- $20 + 4 = 24$
  For 6 plots, she needs 24 logs.

With 24 logs, she could make 6 garden plots.

3. A

Choice A is correct. This number pattern is shrinking by 5. 532, 527, 522, 517

To solve this problem, remember that in a shrinking pattern, the numbers get smaller. The pattern in choice B is a growing pattern not a shrinking pattern.

In the pattern in choice A($532 - 5 = 527$) ($527 - 5 = 522$)($522 - 5 = 517$)

The pattern in choices C and D are also shrinking patterns, but in choice C, the numbers shrink by 10. In choice D, the numbers shrink by 105.

4. C

Choice C is correct.

Start with the first row. Sort all the black shapes into black squares and black circles.

Then, look at the second row. Sort all the white shapes into white squares and white circles.

	Squares	Circles
Black	■ ▪	●
White	▢	◯ ∘

5. 12

Step 1
To solve this addition problem, use the inverse operation of subtraction.
$6 + P = 18$
$P = 18 - 6$
$P = 12$

Step 2
Check by substituting 12 for P.
$6 + P = 18$
$6 + 12 = 18$
The letter P is equal to 12.

SHAPE AND SPACE

Table of Correlations

Outcome		Practice Questions	Unit Test Questions	Practice Test
3SS1.0	Use direct and indirect measurement to solve problems.			
3SS1.1	*Relate the passage of time to common activities, using nonstandard and standard units.*	1, 2	1	21
3SS1.2	*Relate the number of seconds to a minute, the number of minutes to an hour and the number of days to a month in a problem-solving context.*	3, 4	2	22
3SS1.3	Demonstrate an understanding of measuring length.	5, 6, 7	3, 4	
3SS1.4	Demonstrate an understanding of measuring mass.	8, 9	5, 6	23, 24
3SS1.5	Demonstrate an understanding of perimeter of regular and irregular shapes.	10, 11	7	25, 26
3SS2.0	Describe the characteristics of 3-D objects and 2-D shapes, and analyze the relationships among them.			
3SS2.6	*Describe 3-D objects according to the shape of the faces and the number of edges and vertices.*	12, 13, 14	8	27
3SS2.7	*Sort regular and irregular polygons according to the number of sides.*	15, 16	9	28

3SS1.1 Relate the passage of time to common activities, using nonstandard and standard units.

PASSAGE OF TIME

Passage of time is the amount of time between when something begins and when it ends. Passage of time is also the amount of time between events. Passage of time is sometimes called elapsed time.

The passage of time could be short and could be measured in seconds, minutes, or hours. For example, blinking your eye would take only one or two seconds. Going out for recess would take about fifteen minutes. Practising the piano might take one hour. Sleeping through the night could take about 10 hours.

The passage of time could be long and could be measured in days, weeks, months, or years. For example, it might take days to read a chapter book. Swimming lessons could be spread out over several weeks or even months. It might take a child a few years before he or she could learn to ride a bike.

Example

Time can be measured in seconds, minutes, hours, days, weeks, months, or years.

Which measure of time is **best** to measure how long it could take to build a house.

Solution

Step 1
Determine if the time is long or short.
The time is long, so the choices are days, weeks, months, or years.
Step 2
Determine the best measure of time.
It usually takes a long time to build a house. It would probably take at least one year, and often more than one year.

Time can be measured in seconds, minutes, hours, days, weeks, months, or years.

Which measure of time is **best** to measure the time it takes to yawn?

Solution

Step 1
Determine if the time is long or short.
The time is short, so the choices would be seconds or minutes.
Step 2
Determine the best measure of time.
Yawning is a very short event. It would only take seconds to measure.

1. Which of the following units would be **most** appropriate to measure the time it takes an athlete to run 100 m?

   A. Days

   B. Hours

   C. Weeks

   D. Seconds

2. Which of the following units of time **best** measures the time it takes to drive a car from Edmonton to Calgary?

   A. Seconds

   B. Minutes

   C. Hours

   D. Days

3SS1.2 Relate the number of seconds to a minute, the number of minutes to an hour and the number of days to a month in a problem-solving context.

RELATING UNITS OF TIME

Seconds, minutes, hours, days, weeks, and years are some of the units that can be used to measure time.

All the time units are related to each other. This chart shows the relationship between some of the time units.

60 minutes	1 hour
24 hours	1 day
7 days	1 week
52 weeks	1 year

RELATING SECONDS TO MINUTES AND MINUTES TO HOURS

Seconds are very short units of time. There are sixty seconds in one minute.
60 seconds = 1 minute

To find how many seconds there are in two minutes, you need to add 60 + 60. To find how many seconds there are in three minutes, you need to add 60 + 60 + 60.

Hours are longer units of time. There are sixty minutes in one hour.
60 minutes = 1 hour

To find how many minutes there are in two hours, you need to add 60 + 60. To find how many minutes there are in three hours, you need to add 60 + 60 + 60.

Engineering Superhero

www.discover.ualberta.ca

SUPER POWER: Defying Gravity

This beaver can balance on anything — a table corner, your finger, even your nose! In order to defy gravity, he takes advantage of it thanks to the two weights at the end of his superhero cape. His centre of mass is located at the tip of his hat, creating an equilibrium.

To make other great projects like this, come to a DiscoverE summer camp! Visit **www.discover.ualberta.ca** for more info about the DiscoverE engineering and science camps in your community.

INSTRUCTIONS
1. Cut along thick outline.
2. Fold (A) under (B) on dotted line.
3. Fold (C) under cape on dotted line.
4. Fold (B) under cape on dotted line.
5. Tape in place.
6. Fold hat (D) down at a 90° angle.
7. Place the tip of the hat (D) on your fingertip & balance!

FACULTY OF ENGINEERING
UNIVERSITY OF ALBERTA

A member organization of **actua**
Learning for Change.
Pour un monde meilleur
www.actua.ca

DiSCOVERE
www.discover.ualberta.ca

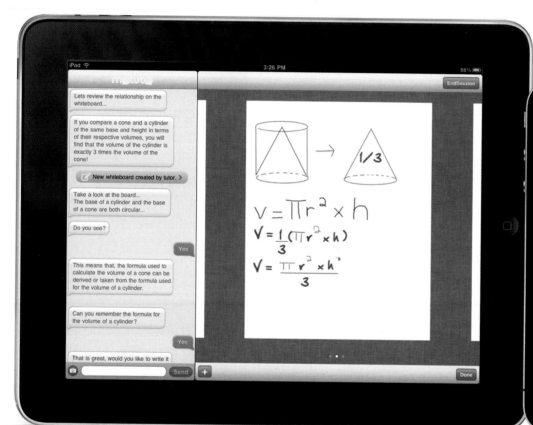

Example

How many minutes are there in four hours?

Solution

Step 1

Recall the number of minutes in one hour.

There are 60 minutes in one hour.

Step 2

Find the number of minutes in four hours.

Add 60 minutes for each of the four hours.

```
  60
  60
  60
+ 60
 240
```

There are 240 minutes in four hours.

RELATING DAYS TO MONTHS

Calendars are charts that show the months of the year, the days of each week, and the dates of all the days. Here is an example of a calendar page.

March						
S	M	T	W	T	F	S
	1	2	3	4	5	6
7	8	9	10	11	12	13
14	15	16	17	18	19	20
21	22	23	24	25	26	27
28	29	30	31			

Each week begins on Sunday. The order of the days is as follows: Sunday, Monday, Tuesday, Wednesday, Thursday, Friday, Saturday. The days of the week repeat their order.

Listed in order, the months are January, February, March, April, May, June, July, August, September, October, November, and December. The months repeat in the same order each year.

This chart shows the number of days in each month.

Months	Days
January	31
February	28
March	31
April	30
May	31
June	30
July	31
August	31
September	30
October	31
November	30
December	31

- April, June, September, and November always have 30 days.
- January, March, May, July, August, October, and December always have 31 days.
- February has 28 days. Every four years, February has 29 days (leap year).

Example

Dick and his family went on a trip. They left home early in the morning on July 5 and came back late at night on July 26.

JULY						
S	**M**	**T**	**W**	**T**	**F**	**S**
1	2	3	4	⑤	6	7
8	9	10	11	12	13	14
15	16	17	18	19	20	21
22	23	24	25	㉖	27	28
29	30	31				

For how many days did the trip last?

Solution

Step 1

Count the number of days for each week of the trip.

Since the family left early in the morning, count the 5th as the first day of the trip. Since the family came back late at night on the 26th, count the 26th as the last day of the trip.

- First week: 3 days
- Second week: 7 days
- Third week: 7 days
- Fourth week: 5 days

Step 2

Add the number of days for each week that the family was on the trip.

$3 + 7 + 7 + 5 = 22$

The trip lasted for 22 days.

---

3. Grandpa walked 5 km in 2 h. How many minutes did it take him to walk that distance?

    A. 60 min   B. 90 min

    C. 120 min   D. 150 min

Use the following information to answer the next question.

Susan is excited because her grandmother is coming to stay with the family for a long visit. Her grandmother will arrive early in the morning of October 15. She will leave to go home in the evening of December 2.

Numerical Response

4. For how many days will Susan's grandmother visit the family? _____

3SS1.3 Demonstrate an understanding of measuring length.

ESTIMATING, MEASURING, AND RECORDING LENGTH

Centimetres and metres are two units that are commonly used to measure length.
The length (l) of an object is how long it is, the width (w) is how wide it is, and the height (h) is how tall it is.

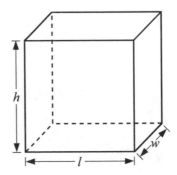

ESTIMATING LENGTH

When you estimate length, you are not looking for an exact measure. You can estimate the length of an object by using a referent. A referent is any object that has about the same length as a particular standard unit of measure like a centimetre (cm) or a metre (m).

A referent for a centimetre could be the width of your finger. Your finger is approximately one centimetre wide.

A referent for a metre could be the distance from the tip of your middle finger on your left hand to the tip of your middle finger on your right hand when your arms are stretched out. The distance between your fingertips is about one metre.

Example

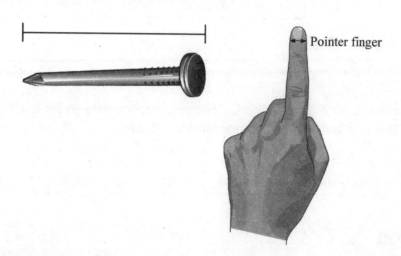

Pointer finger

Estimate the length of the nail by using the width of your pointer finger as a referent for 1 cm.

Solution

It would take about five finger widths to measure the length of the nail.

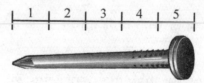

Therefore, the nail is about 5 cm long.

MEASURING LENGTH

Rulers, measuring tapes, and metre sticks are some of the tools used to measure shorter lengths, heights, and distances. When using any of these tools, it is important to start measuring from the correct line at the beginning of the tool used.

Example

Sarah uses a centimetre ruler to measure the length of her pencil, as shown in the picture.

How long is Sarah's pencil?

Solution

To read the ruler, notice where the tip of the pencil comes to on the ruler. The eraser is at 0 cm. The opposite tip of the pencil is at 15 cm.

Sarah's pencil is 15 cm long.

DRAWING LINES

To draw a line of a specific length, remember to start at zero, the first line on the ruler. Put the tip of the pencil at the zero. Then, following the straight edge of the ruler, draw the line until you reach the number for the length you require. Draw carefully to make sure your line is the proper length.

Example

Each student is given a paper with a picture of this pencil on it.

Draw a line that is 3 cm longer than the pencil shown.

Solution

To measure for a line 3 cm longer than the pencil shown, line up your ruler at the end of the pencil tip.

Make a tick at the 3 cm line.

Take another ruler, and draw a line starting from the tip of the eraser. Draw the line until you reach the 3 cm tick on the ruler.

This picture shows a line that is 3 cm longer than the pencil.

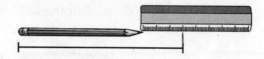

Use the following information to answer the next question.

Ruby draws a picture of herself in art class.

5. What is the height of Ruby's picture?

   A. 5 cm

   B. 6 cm

   C. 8 cm

   D. 9 cm

Use the following information to answer the next question.

Height

The given shape is a rectangle.

Numerical Response

6. Measured with a ruler, the height of the rectangle is _____ cm.

Use the following information to answer the next question.

One cat rests on the top of a climbing pole. Another cat stands at the base of the climbing pole.

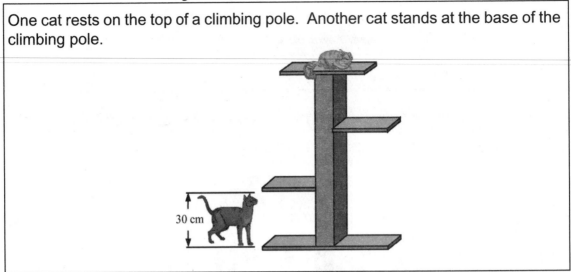

Written Response

7. About how high off the floor is the cat on the top of the climbing pole?

3SS1.4 Demonstrate an understanding of measuring mass.

MASS

Mass is a measure of how heavy or how light an object is. Mass is often measured in grams (g) or kilograms (kg). A gram is about as heavy as a jelly bean, and a kilogram is about as heavy as a textbook.

ESTIMATING MASS

To estimate how heavy something is, look at how big the object is and what it is made of. For example, a cookie is a small object, so it will have a small mass. Think about the mass of another object, such as a jelly bean. Then, think about how many jelly beans will equal the mass of the cookie.

Example

What is a good estimate of the mass of a chicken egg?

Solution

Step 1

Choose the best measure of mass.

The best measure to estimate the mass of an egg is grams. Kilograms are used to measure heavier items.

Step 2

Estimate the mass.

To estimate the mass of an egg, use a referent for a gram. One referent you can use is a jelly bean or a small paper clip.

You need to know how many jelly beans will weigh the same as the egg. Hold the jelly beans in one hand and the egg in the other hand. Have a friend keep adding jelly beans to the one hand until both hands seem to be holding the same weight. A good guess is that it will take about 25 jelly beans to equal the mass of the egg.

A good estimate for the mass of a chicken egg is 25 grams.

MEASURING MASS

The mass of an object can be found using a weighing scale or a balance scale.

To use a weighing scale, place the object on the scale and read its mass on the dial or display.

To use a balance scale, place the objects on either side of the scale. When the scale is balanced, the objects on both sides have the same mass.

Example

Frankie wants to determine the mass of the candle. He uses a balance scale to measure the actual mass of the candle.

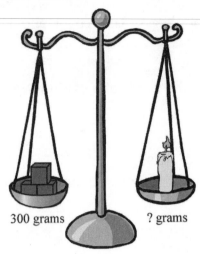

300 grams   ? grams

What is the mass of the candle?

Solution

The candle and the three blocks balance the scale. The picture shows that the three blocks have a mass of 300 g.

Therefore, the candle has a mass of 300 g.

RELATING GRAMS TO KILOGRAMS

Grams and kilograms are related to each other.
1 000 grams = 1 kilogram

To find out how many grams there are in three kilograms, add 1 000 grams three times.
1 000 g + 1 000 g + 1 000 g
= 3 000 g
= 3 kg

Example

Jasmine bought a bag of sugar and a bag of flour.

FLOUR
3 kg

SUGAR
2 kg

In grams, what is the total mass of the bags that Jasmine bought?

Solution

Step 1
Calculate the mass of the bags in kilograms.
Add the two masses.
3 + 2 = 5
The mass of the two bags is 5 kg.

Step 2
Determine the mass in grams.
Since 1 kg = 1 000 g, then 5 kg = 5 000 g.
The mass of the bags in grams is 5 000 g.

---

8. Mrs. Smith bought 3 kilograms of jellybeans for a party. How many grams of jellybeans did Mrs. Smith buy?

    A. 300 grams   B. 330 grams

    C. 3 000 grams   D. 3 300 grams

Use the following information to answer the next question.

One side of the scale in the diagram holds a 3 kg mass. The other side of the scale holds a 1 kg mass and a kitten.

3 kg   1 kg

Numerical Response

9. What is the mass of the kitten in the diagram? _____

3SS1.5 Demonstrate an understanding of perimeter of regular and irregular shapes.

PERIMETER

Perimeter is the distance around the outside of a shape.

ESTIMATING PERIMETER

To estimate the perimeter of a shape, use what you already know about estimating lengths and distances.

For example, you know that the width of your finger or the width of a die is about 1 cm. You can use a finger width or a die as a referent to estimate the distance around a small shape.

Example

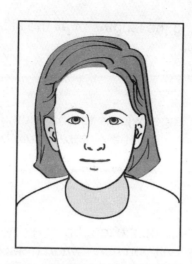

Erika has this picture of her friend Melissa. She wants to put a lace trim around the picture. To do this, she needs to know the perimeter of the picture.

Using a referent, estimate the perimeter of the picture.

Solution

Step 1
Estimate the width of the picture using a referent.
One referent you can use is the width of your pointer finger.

Pointer finger

Place your finger at the bottom left corner of the picture. Count how many finger widths it takes to go across the width of the picture.

Depending on how wide your finger is, it could take about five finger widths, which is about 5 cm.

Step 2
Estimate the height of the picture using the width of your finger as a referent.

Place your finger at the bottom right corner of the picture, and see how many finger widths it takes to go up the height of the picture.

Depending on how wide your finger is, it could take about seven finger widths, which is about 7 cm.

Step 3

Find the perimeter by adding the lengths of all the sides together.

You can use the formula

$P = l + w + l + w$

$= 5 + 7 + 5 + 7$.

$= 24$

If your estimation was five finger widths for the width and seven finger widths for the height, the estimated perimeter of the picture would be 24 cm.

MEASURING PERIMETER

To find the perimeter of a shape, add the lengths of all the sides together. When you write perimeter, be sure to write the unit you used when measuring the lengths.

Example

A rectangular garden has a length of 12 m and a width of 5 m.

What is the perimeter of the garden?

Solution

Find the perimeter of a shape by adding the lengths (12 m) and the widths (5 m) of the garden.

$12 + 5 + 12 + 5 = 34$

The perimeter of the garden is 34 m.

CONSTRUCTING SHAPES FOR A GIVEN PERIMETER

You can construct a shape when you are given a perimeter. It is possible to draw several different shapes that all have the same perimeter.

Example

On the grid shown, draw three different rectangles that each have a perimeter of 12 units. Label the side lengths of each rectangle.

For this assignment, if a rectangle is flipped, it is not considered to be a different rectangle.

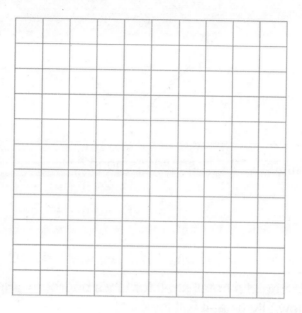

Solution

There are three different rectangles that could each have a perimeter of 12 units.

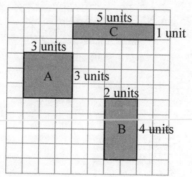

Jake draws a diagram of the school's new baseball diamond. Each side of the diamond is 12 m long.

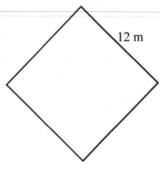

12 m

10. What is the perimeter of the baseball diamond?

A. 12 m

B. 24 m

C. 36 m

D. 48 m

Use the following information to answer the next question.

Lily's dad plans to build a small shelf for Lily's bedroom. He draws a diagram on grid paper to show Lily what it will look like.

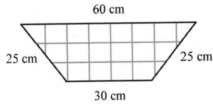

60 cm

25 cm   25 cm

30 cm

Written Response

11. What is the perimeter of the shelf?

3SS2.6 Describe 3-D objects according to the shape of the faces and the number of edges and vertices.

THREE-DIMENSIONAL OBJECTS

Three-dimensional (3-D) objects are objects that have dimensions of width, length, and depth. These give an object its form. Some examples of 3-D objects are pyramids, prisms, cones, spheres, and cylinders.

PYRAMIDS AND PRISMS

Pyramids and prisms are named by the shape of their bases. Some possible shapes of a base can be a triangle, a rectangle, or a square.

A pyramid is a solid made up of one base in the shape of a polygon. The faces of a pyramid are triangular, and they meet at one point called the vertex.

Vertex

For example, the following objects are pyramids. A pyramid is named by the shape of its base.

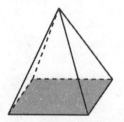

Rectangular-based pyramid   *Triangular-based pyramid*

Square-based pyramid

A prism is a solid made up of two parallel bases of the same size and shape. The bases are shaded in the following prisms. A prism is named by the shape of its base

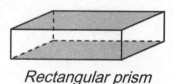
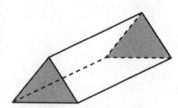

Square prism

Rectangular prism

Triangular prism

FACES, EDGES, AND VERTICES

A face is any flat surface on a prism or pyramid. A face is described using the name of its two-dimensional shape, which could be a triangle, a square, or a rectangle. An edge is where any two faces meet. A vertex is where at least three edges come together. The edges form a corner or point at the vertex.

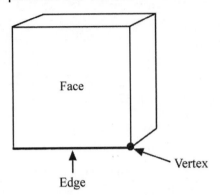

This chart describes some of the most common three-dimensional objects.

Name of 3-D Object	Number of Faces	Shape of Faces (2-D)	Number of Edges	Number of Vertices
Cube or rectangular prism	6	6 squares or 6 rectangles	12	8
Triangular prism	5	2 triangles, 3 rectangles	9	6
Square-based pyramid	5	1 square, 4 triangles	8	5
Triangular-based pyramid	4	4 triangles	6	4
Pentagonal-based pyramid	6	1 pentagon, 5 triangles	10	6

Example

This is a picture of a three-dimensional object.

Square
prism

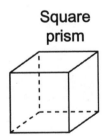

Determine the number of faces, vertices, and edges the given object has.

Solution

Step 1

Count the number of faces.

A face is any flat surface on a prism or pyramid.

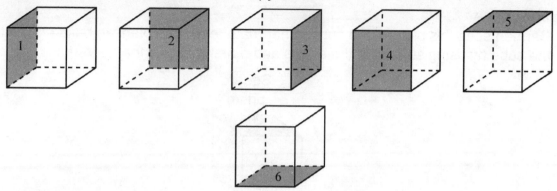

The object has 6 faces.

Step 2

Count the number of edges.

An edge is where any two faces meet.

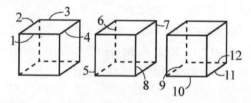

The object has 12 edges.

Step 3

Count the number of vertices.

A vertex is where at least three edges meet. The edges form a corner or point at the vertex.

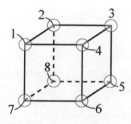

The object has 8 vertices.

The object has 6 faces, 12 edges, and 8 vertices.

CONSTRUCTING THREE-DIMENSIONAL OBJECTS

You can construct a model or a skeleton of a 3-D object to help you understand it. The skeleton shows how many faces, edges, and vertices the object has, as well as the shape of the faces. You can use different materials, such as straws and marshmallows or modelling clay and toothpicks, to construct a skeleton.

Example

Carmen sees this picture of a cube in her math text. She plans to build a skeleton of the cube by using straws for the edges and marshmallows for the vertices.

Square prism

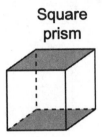

Explain how Carmen can make a skeleton of a cube using straws and marshmallows.

Solution

Step 1

Determine the number of straws needed.

An edge is where two faces meet.

A cube has 12 edges: 4 at the top, 4 at the bottom, and 4 on the sides.

Carmen will need 12 straws, one for each edge.

Step 2

Determine the number of marshmallows needed.

A vertex is where edges meet.

A cube has 8 vertices: 4 at the top and 4 at the bottom.

Carmen will need 8 marshmallows, one for each vertex.

Step 3
Construct the skeleton.

1. Make a square with 4 straws and 4 marshmallows. This will make the bottom skeleton base.
2. Place a straw up and down into each of the four marshmallows. These straws will form the skeleton side edges.
3. Place a marshmallow on top of each vertical straw. These marshmallows will form the top vertices.
4. Place a straw between every two top marshmallows. This will make the top skeleton base.

This diagram shows what the skeleton cube will look like.

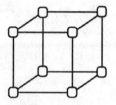

Use the following information to answer the next question.

Lewis saw a carnival tent that had the shape shown here.

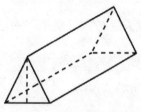

12. The number of faces, edges, and vertices the given shape has is
   A. 7 faces, 9 edges, and 7 vertices
   B. 6 faces, 3 edges, and 6 vertices
   C. 5 faces, 9 edges, and 6 vertices
   D. 5 faces, 4 edges, and 5 vertices

Use the following information to answer the next question.

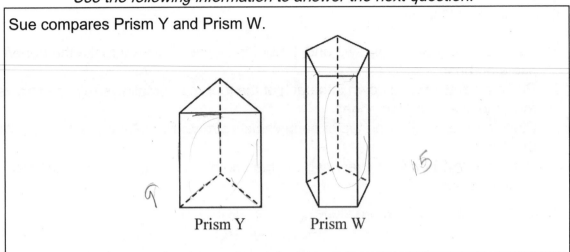

Sue compares Prism Y and Prism W.

Prism Y   Prism W

13. How many more edges does Prism W have than Prism Y?

    A. 4   B. 5

    C. 6   D. 7

Numerical Response

14. How many edges does a cube have? _____

3SS2.7 Sort regular and irregular polygons according to the number of sides.

POLYGONS

Polygons are figures that have many sides. They can be sorted by the number of sides they have.

In a **regular polygon**, all the sides are equal in length.

Regular polygons

Class Focus   114   Castle Rock Research

For example, the shapes in this chart are regular polygons.

Name	Shape	Number of Sides
Triangle	△	3
Quadrilateral	□	4
Pentagon	⬠	5
Hexagon	⬡	6
Heptagon	⬡	7
Octagon	⯃	8

In an **irregular polygon**, all the sides are not equal in length.

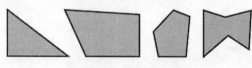

Irregular polygons

A ruler can be used to measure the length of sides to determine if a polygon is regular or irregular.

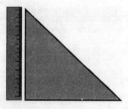

Example

Draw 2 polygons that each have 3 sides. Make one a regular polygon and make one an irregular polygon. Be sure to label each figure. Explain your work.

Solution

Example answers:

Regular polygon:

A regular polygon has all equal side lengths, so I drew a triangle that has all three sides that are equal in length.

An irregular polygon:

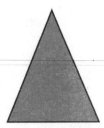

An irregular polygon does not have all its sides with equal lengths, so I drew a triangle with two equal length sides, but the third side is not the same length.

---

15. Which of the following irregular polygons is a pentagon?

A. 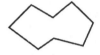   B.

C.    D.

16. Which of the following shapes is **not** an irregular polygon?

A.    B.

C.   D.

ANSWERS AND SOLUTIONS
SHAPE AND SPACE

1. D	5. B	9. 2 kg	13. C
2. C	6. 2	10. D	14. 12
3. C	7. WR	11. WR	15. C
4. 49	8. C	12. C	16. A

1. D

Step 1
Examine each unit of time.

- Days and weeks are very large units of time. It would not take days or weeks to run 100 m.
- Hours may be used to measure the time taken to complete very long races, like 50 km. However, 100 m is a short distance to run and would not take very long.
- Seconds could be used to time a short-distance run. An athlete could probably run 100 m in several seconds (or minutes, but minutes is not a unit listed in the alternatives).

Step 2
Select the most appropriate unit.
Of the alternatives listed, the most appropriate unit of time in which to measure how long it takes an athlete to run 100 m is seconds.

2. C

Step 1
Examine each option.

- Seconds are a very small unit of time, so the number of seconds would be huge.
- Minutes are a larger unit of time but still too small to measure a long time period.
- Hours are a larger unit of time and would be more practical to use.
- Days are a very large unit of time (24 hours) to measure a trip of that distance.

Step 2
Select the best option.
The best and most practical unit of time to measure the trip from Edmonton to Calgary is hours.

3. C

Step 1
Determine the number of minutes in one hour.
60 min = 1 h

Step 2
Calculate the number of minutes in two hours.
60 + 60 = 120
It took Grandpa 120 min to walk 5 km.

4. 49

Step 1
Count the number of days.
Use the calendar pages to count the number of days for each month that Susan's grandmother will visit.
Remember to count the first and last days of the visit.

- October 15 to October 31→ 17 days
- November 1 to November 30→ 30 days
- December 1 to December 2→ 2 days

Step 2
Calculate the number of days.
Add the three numbers together.
17 + 30 + 2 = 49
Susan's grandmother will visit the family for 49 days.

5. B

Place your ruler on the dark line on the left or right side of the picture. Line up the 0 with the little end line. The other end line will line up with the 6 on your ruler.

Ruby's picture is 6 cm high.

6. 2

Step 1

Place a centimetre ruler at the bottom of the rectangle.

Line up the edge of the rectangle with the 0 on the ruler.

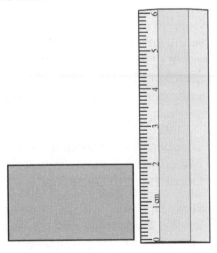

Step 2

Count the centimetres.

Start at 0, and count the centimetres up to the mark that lines up with the top of the rectangle.

0, 1 cm, 2 cm

The height of the rectangle is 2 cm.

7. WR

Step 1

Identify the height of the cat at the base of the climbing pole.

The height of the cat standing at the base of the climbing pole is 30 cm.

Step 2

Use the height of the cat as a referent.

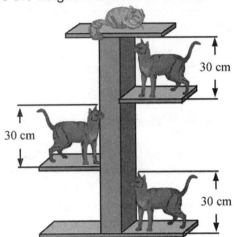

The distance between the base of the climbing pole and the first shelf is the same as the height of the cat.

Since there are 3 shelves, the height of 3 cats is a good estimate of the height of the climbing pole. Add the heights of 3 cats to find the height of the climbing pole.
30 cm + 30 cm + 30 cm = 90 cm

The cat at the top of the climbing pole is about 90 cm off the floor.

8. C

Choice C is correct. Mrs. Smith bought 3 000 grams of jellybeans.

Think:

1 kg = 1 000 g
2 kg = 2 000 g
3 kg = 3 000 g

9. 2 kg

The kitten has a mass of 2 kg.

When the two sides of a balance scale are even with each other (balanced), the two sides have equal masses. That means that the 1 kg mass and the mass of the kitten are equal to 3 kg.

If *k* represents the mass of the kitten, you could use this equation to find the answer.

$3 = 1 + k$

$3 - 1 = k$

$k = 2$

Your answer is correct if it has the unit of measure (kg) written after the number.

10. **D**

Choice D is correct. The perimeter of the baseball diamond is 48 m.

Add the lengths of the four sides together to find the perimeter.

12 m + 12 m + 12 m + 12 m = 48 m

11. **WR**

Add the lengths of all sides of the shelf.

25 + 25 + 60 + 30 = 140

The perimeter is 140 cm.

12. **C**

Step 1

Count the number of faces.

There are 5 faces.

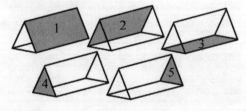

Step 2

Count the number of edges.

There are 9 edges.

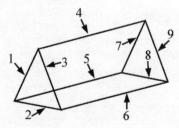

Step 3

Count the number of vertices.

There are 6 vertices.

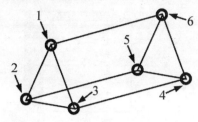

The given shape has 5 faces, 9 edges, and 6 vertices.

13. **C**

Choice C is correct. Prism W has six more edges than Prism Y.

An edge is the line that forms where two faces meet.

Prism Y has 9 edges, and Prism W has 15 edges.

Subtract 9 from 15 (15 – 9 = 6).

14. **12**

Step 1

Recall what a cube is.

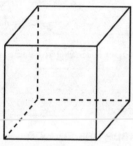

A cube is a 3-D figure made out of six square faces.

Step 2
Recall what an edge is.

An edge is formed when two faces meet.

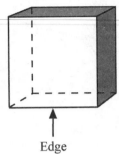

Edge

Count the number of edges. There are four top edges, four side edges, and four bottom edges.

A cube has 12 edges.

15. C

Step 1
Recall that a pentagon is a polygon that has five sides.

Step 2
Count the number of sides that each shape has.

This shape has eight sides.

This shape has six sides.

This shape has five sides.

This shape has six sides.

This irregular polygon is a pentagon.

16. A

Step 1
Determine the difference between a regular polygon and an irregular polygon.

- In a regular polygon, all the sides have the same length.
- In an irregular polygon, the sides do **not** all have the same length.

Step 2
Identify the shape that has equal side lengths.

The square has four equal side lengths.

UNIT TEST — SHAPE AND SPACE

1. The time it takes Andy to complete a 42 km race is **best** recorded in which of the following units?

    A. Seconds
    B. Minutes
    C. Hours
    D. Days

2. How many minutes are there between 8:30 A.M. and 2:30 P.M.?

    A. 300 minutes
    B. 360 minutes
    C. 400 minutes
    D. 420 minutes

Use the following information to answer the next question.

This tire is 3 metres high. There is a man standing beside the tire.

3. About how tall is the man?

    A. Less than 1 m
    B. 1 m
    C. 2 m
    D. 3 m

Use the following information to answer the next question.

Sam's teacher asked him to measure this pen in math class.

4. What is the length of the pen?

    A. 9 cm
    B. 10 cm
    C. 11 cm
    D. 12 cm

Use the following information to answer the next question.

Leela put an orange with a mass of 50 grams on one side of a balance scale. She then put an apple on the other side of the scale. Leela then estimated the mass of the apple.

50 grams

? grams

5. Which of the following masses is the **best** estimate of the mass of the apple?

   A. 48 grams   B. 55 grams

   C. 58 grams   D. 60 grams

6. Elsa measured and recorded the masses of four objects in her classroom. Which of the following objects **most likely** has a mass of 40 grams?

   A. Straw   B. Glue stick

   C. Basketball   D. Math textbook

7. In art class, four students made frames for pictures they painted. Which of the following frames has a perimeter of 66 cm?

  A.

15 cm

19 cm

  B.
17 cm

18 cm

  C.
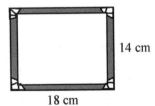
14 cm

18 cm

  D.
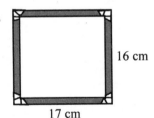
16 cm

17 cm

Use the following information to answer the next question.

Each of the given figures shows a rectangular prism.

8. How many faces, vertices, and edges do all rectangular prisms have?
    A. 4 faces, 8 vertices, and 12 edges   B. 6 faces, 8 vertices, and 12 edges
    C. 6 faces, 12 vertices, and 8 edges   D. 5 faces, 8 vertices, and 10 edges

9. Which of the following polygons has the **least** number of sides?
    A. Square   B. Triangle
    C. Hexagon   D. Pentagon

ANSWERS AND SOLUTIONS — UNIT TEST

1. C	4. C	7. D
2. B	5. A	8. B
3. C	6. B	9. B

1. C

Step 1
Examine each unit of time.

- Seconds and minutes are too small to measure the time it would take to run 42 km. Andy may be able to run 1 km in about 10 to 20 minutes, depending on how fast he runs.
- Days are too large a unit, since there are 24 hours in a day.
- It would take a person several hours to run 42 km.

Step 2
Select the most appropriate unit.
Of the alternatives listed, the most appropriate unit of time to measure how long it would take to run 42 km is hours.

2. B

Step 1
Count the number of hours between 8:30 A.M. and 2:30 P.M.
Start with 8:30, and count by 1s as you pass each hour.
8:30, 9:30(1), 10:30(2), 11:30(3), 12:30(4), 1:30(5), 2:30(6).
There are six hours between 8:30 A.M. and 2:30 P.M.

Step 2
Determine the number of minutes in six hours.
60 minutes = 1 hour
Add 60 to itself 6 times.
60 + 60 + 60 + 60 + 60 + 60 = 360
There are 360 minutes between 8:30 A.M. and 2:30 P.M.

3. C

Choice C is correct.

Since the tire on the truck is 3 metres high, divide the height into 3 equal parts.
Each part represents 1 metre in height.
The height of the man reaches to about the second part. The man is about 2 m tall.

4. C

Choice C is correct. The pen is 11 cm long.

One tip of the pen is right at the 0.
The opposite tip of the pen is at the 11.
That means the pen is 11 cm long.

5. A

Choice A is correct. The best estimate of the mass of the apple is 48 grams.

The side of the balance scale with the apple is higher than the side with the orange.
This means that the apple has a mass that is less than the mass of the orange. Of the given masses, only 48 is less than 50.

6. B

A glue stick would most likely have a mass of 40 grams.

One straw most likely has a mass of just a few grams. Both a basketball and a math textbook would most likely have much greater masses.

7. D

Choice D is correct.

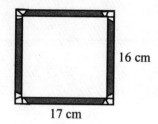

To find the perimeter, add the lengths of all four sides.

16 + 16 + 17 + 17 = 66

You could also multiply each of the given side lengths by 2 and then add the products.

16 × 2 = 32
17 × 2 = 34
32 + 34 = 66

8. B

Choice B is correct. All rectangular prisms have 6 faces, 8 vertices, and 12 edges.

9. B

Choice B is correct. A triangle has the least number of sides.

A square has four sides, a triangle has three sides, a pentagon has five sides, and a hexagon has six sides.

NOTES

Statistics and Probability

STATISTICS AND PROBABILITY

Table of Correlations

	Outcome	Practice Questions	Unit Test Questions	Practice Test
3SP1.0	Collect, display and analyze data to solve problems.			
3SP1.1	Collect first-hand data and organize it to answer questions.	1, 2	1	29
3SP1.2	Construct, label and interpret bar graphs to solve problems.	3, 4, 5	2, 3	30

3SP1.1 Collect first-hand data and organize it to answer questions.

COLLECTING AND ORGANIZING DATA

People have questions about many different topics every day. Sometimes, they can find answers by asking questions, observing events, or taking measurements. Asking the right question is important for collecting the correct information.

Example

Dawn is conducting a survey of her classmates. She wants to know the school subject each of them likes best.

What would be a good question for Dawn to ask her classmates?

Solution

A good question would be to simply ask them what their favourite school subject is.

Dawn needs to match the information she wants to collect to the wording of the question she asks. Since Dawn wants to learn what school subject her classmates like best, she needs to ask a question about that. If she wanted, she could even give specific choices and ask if their favourite subject is math, science, language arts, social studies, art, music, or physical education.

Tally charts, checklists, and line plots are some of the many methods used to record data. Checklists organize information by using check marks to indicate a choice. To record the frequency of something occurring, you can use a tally mark in a tally chart. Tallies are usually bundled into groups of five to make counting easier.

Example

Kasar surveyed his friends to see what flavour ice cream they liked best. He gave them four choices: chocolate, vanilla, orange, cherry.

He recorded the data he collected in this chart.

Name	Favourite Flavour
Tim	Chocolate
Jordan	Vanilla
Robbie	Cherry
Keira	Chocolate
Jody	Orange
Franco	Vanilla
Jasmine	Cherry
Chung	Orange
Dillon	Chocolate
Zara	Vanilla

Create a tally chart to display the data Kasar collected.

Solution

Step 1

Set up the tally chart.

List the flavours of ice cream in one column. Create a second column for the tallies.

Flavour	Tally
Cherry	
Chocolate	
Orange	
Vanilla	

Step 2

Fill in the tally chart.

Make a line or tally for each friend's favourite ice cream choice. Start with the first person on the list (Tim) and work your way down the list. Be careful not to miss anyone.

This tally chart displays the data Kasar collected.

Flavour	Tally
Cherry	||
Chocolate	|||
Orange	||
Vanilla	|||

- Two friends chose cherry.
- Three friends chose chocolate.
- Two friends chose orange.
- Three friends chose vanilla.

Sometimes, you will need to answer questions about data that is presented in lists, tally charts, or line plots. Look carefully at the data presented to answer the questions correctly.

Example

Mr. Hendry asked his Grade 3 students what their favourite winter sport was. The tally chart shows the data he gathered.

Sport	Number of Students
Tobogganing	卌				
Downhill skiing	卌	
Cross-country skiing			
skidooing	卌			
Skating	卌

How many students took part in the survey?

Solution

To figure out how many students took part in the survey, total up the number of students who voted for each sport.
9 + 6 + 2 + 8 + 5 = 30

There were 30 students who took part in the survey.

What is the favourite winter sport of the Grade 3 students?

Solution

The favourite winter sport is the one that the greatest number of students chose.

Look at the number of students who chose each sport:

- Nine students chose tobogganing.
- Six students chose downhill skiing.
- Two students chose cross-country skiing.
- Eight students chose skidooing.
- Five students chose skating.

Tobogganing is the favourite winter sport of the Grade 3 students.

How many more students chose tobogganing than cross-country skiing?

Solution

Find the difference between the number of students who chose tobogganing (9) and the number of students who chose cross-country skiing (2).
9 − 2 = 7

Seven more students chose tobogganing than cross-country skiing.

Use the following information to answer the next question.

Rio's class collected mittens, hats, scarves, and jackets for children in need. They displayed the number of items they collected on a line plot and in a chart.

Warm Clothes Collection

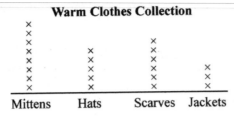

Item	Number Collected
Mittens	8
Hats	5
Scarves	6
Jackets	3

1. Which item was collected the **least**?

   A. Hats   B. Mittens

   C. Scarves   D. Jackets

Use the following information to answer the next question.

Julia surveys ten friends to find what their favourite colours are. She writes the data she collects beside each person's name.

Name	Favourite Colour
Christine	Yellow
Jordan	Yellow
Amelia	Green
Keira	Blue
Lily	Red
Lauren	Yellow
Claire	Blue
Morgan	Red
Faith	Green
Sophia	Blue

Julia then makes a tally chart to display the results.

2. Which tally chart correctly shows the number of students who chose each colour?

A.

Colour	Tally
Red	|||
Yellow	||
Blue	||
Green	|||

B.

Colour	Tally
Red	||
Yellow	|||
Blue	|||
Green	||

C.

Colour	Tally
Red	||
Yellow	|||
Blue	||
Green	|||

D.

Colour	Tally
Red	|||
Yellow	||
Blue	|||
Green	||

3SP1.2 Construct, label and interpret bar graphs to solve problems.

Bar Graphs

A graph is used to organize and display data. The main purpose of a graph is to present information clearly so it can be compared.

CONSTRUCTING BAR GRAPHS

Bar graphs are graphs that use bars to show quantities. When you construct a bar graph, you must include a title, labels along the **x-axis** and the **y-axis**, and bars to represent the data you want to show.

Example

The parents of students in grades 1 to 3 at Lennon Elementary School completed a survey. They wanted to find out their children's favourite burger places. The results are shown in this chart.

Restaurant	Number of Students
Mings	30
Ahmed and Williams	25
Marissa's	15
King Burger	10

Draw a bar graph showing the data in the given chart.

Solution

Step 1

Label the parts of the graph.

To display the burger places in a bar graph, start by writing a title for the graph. Then, label the *x*-axis and the *y*-axis.

A good title for the bar graph might be "Favourite Place for Burgers."

Label the *x*-axis "Restaurant." The *x*-axis is the axis along the bottom of the graph.

Label the *y*-axis "Number of students." The *y*-axis is the axis on the side of the graph.

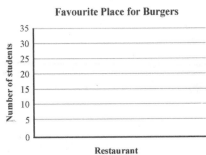

Favourite Place for Burgers

Step 2

Draw the bars that represent the data.

Start with the first restaurant in the chart, Mings. Since 30 students chose Mings as their favourite burger place, draw the bar up to 30 on the *y*-axis.

Then, draw the bar for the next restaurant, Ahmed and Williams. Since 25 students chose that restaurant, draw the bar up to 25.

Draw the bar for Marissa's to 15 and the bar for King Burger to 10.

This bar graph represents the data found in the survey.

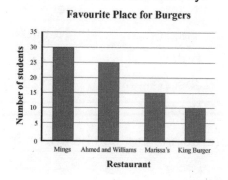

DRAWING CONCLUSIONS

Data in bar graphs can be compared and used to help you draw conclusions.

Look carefully at the information presented in the graph. Use the information to answer questions and see what is important. Compare the bars in the bar graph to give you the information you need. Evaluate all the data given in order to draw your conclusion.

Example

This bar graph shows the height in centimetres of four boys. The boys are Henry, Joseph, Patrick, and Thomas.

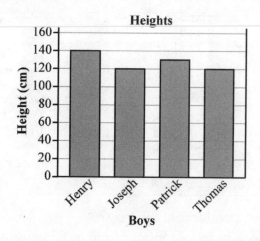

What conclusion about the heights of the boys can be drawn from the bar graph shown?

Solution

A conclusion is a statement about the data that has not already been presented. You can make a chart to help you understand the data and draw your conclusion.

The top of each bar shows how tall each boy is. If you order the heights from tallest to shortest and place them in a table, it may be easier to evaluate the data.

Name	Height (cm)
Henry	140
Patrick	130
Joseph	120
Thomas	120

Here are some of the conclusions that can be drawn from the graph:

1. Henry is the tallest boy measured.
2. Joseph is 20 cm shorter than Henry.
3. Joseph and Thomas are the same height and the shortest boys measured.
4. Patrick is 10 cm shorter than Henry and 10 cm taller than Joseph and Thomas.

Use the following information to answer the next question.

The bar graph shows how many chapter books a Grade 3 class read each month from September to January.

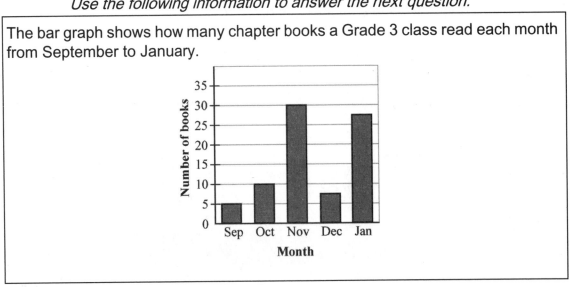

3. Which of the following statements is **true**?
   A. Fewer books were read in January than in November.
   B. Two times more books were read in November than October.
   C. Two times more books were read in December than September.
   D. The same number of books were read in October and December.

Use the following information to answer the next question.

Kenton asks some students at his school what their favourite activity is. He makes a bar graph to show the results.

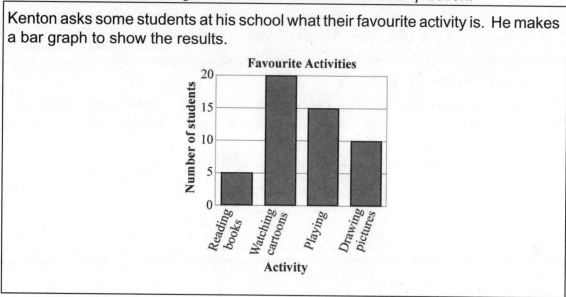

4. Which of the following statements is **true**?

   A. More students chose reading books than playing.

   B. Fewer students chose playing than drawing pictures.

   C. Fewer students chose watching cartoons than playing.

   D. More students chose drawing pictures than reading books.

Use the following information to answer the next question.

Cathy counts the number of crayons in the art box. There are 4 red crayons, 7 green crayons, 5 blue crayons, and 2 yellow crayons.

Written Response

5. Draw a bar graph using the grid below to show the number of each colour of crayons Cathy found in the art box. One square will represent two crayons. Remember to use appropriate labels and a title.

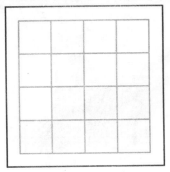

ANSWERS AND SOLUTIONS
STATISTICS AND PROBABILITY

1. D	3. A	5. WR
2. B	4. D	

1. D

The chart and line plot show that the class collected 8 pairs of mittens, 5 hats, 6 scarves, and 3 jackets.

The item that the class collected the least was jackets.

2. B

Choice B is correct.

Two people chose red (Lily and Morgan). Three people chose yellow (Christine, Jordan, and Lauren). Three people chose blue (Keira, Claire, and Sophia). Two people chose green (Amelia and Faith).

Colour	Tally
Red	I I
Yellow	I I I
Blue	I I I
Green	I I

3. A

Choice A is correct. Fewer books were read in January than in November.

About 27 books were read in January, but 30 books were read in November.
The number 27 is less than the number 30.

4. D

More students chose drawing pictures than reading books.

Ten students chose drawing pictures, and five students chose reading books. Ten is greater than five.

5. WR

Step
Label the parts of the graph.
To display the crayons in a bar graph, start by writing a title for the graph. Then, label the x-axis and the y-axis.
A good title for the bar graph might be "Crayons in Art Box."
Label the x-axis "Number of crayons." The x-axis is the axis along the bottom of the graph.
Label the y-axis "Colours." The y-axis is the axis on the side of the graph

Step
Draw the bars that represent the data.
Start with the first colour in the chart, yellow. Since 2 crayons were yellow, draw the bar across to 2 on the x-axis.
Then, draw the bar for the next colour, blue. Since 5 crayons were blue, draw the bar across to 5.
Draw the bar for green to 7 and the bar for red to 4.
This bar graph represents the crayons in the box.

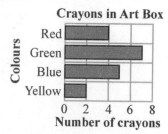

Crayons in Art Box

UNIT TEST — STATISTICS AND PROBABILITY

Use the following information to answer the next question.

Ryan collected the following data from the students in his class. He used tallies to record the data he collected.

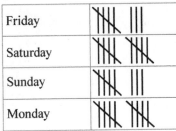

Friday	⊬Ⅱ Ⅲ
Saturday	⊬Ⅱ ⊬Ⅱ
Sunday	⊬Ⅱ Ⅲ
Monday	⊬Ⅱ ⊬Ⅱ

1. Which of the following questions did Ryan **most likely** ask the students?
   A. Which month do you like best?
   B. Which holiday do you like best?
   C. Which season do you like best?
   D. Which day of the week do you like best?

Use the following information to answer the next question.

Tara asked everyone in her class what type of pets they had. She then made this graph to show the data she collected.

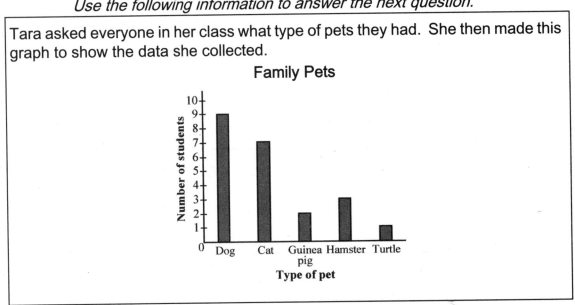

2. Which of the following conclusions can be drawn about the type of pets the students had?
   A. Cats are more popular than dogs.
   B. Cats are less popular than hamsters.
   C. Guinea pigs are less popular than turtles.
   D. Hamsters are more popular then guinea pigs.

Use the following information to answer the next question.

For Earth Day, one class at Williamson Elementary School voted to do a project. This chart shows the number of votes that each project received.

Project	Number of Votes
Juice box recycling	‖‖ ‖‖ ‖‖ I
Worm composting	‖‖ I I I
Car-pooling to school	I I
Picking up garbage	I I I I

3. When the number of votes are ordered from least to greatest, the order of the projects is

   A. juice box recycling, worm composting, car-pooling to school, and picking up garbage

   B. juice box recycling, worm composting, picking up garbage, and car-pooling to school

   C. car-pooling to school, picking up garbage, worm composting, and juice box recycling

   D. picking up garbage, juice box recycling, worm composting, and car-pooling to school

ANSWERS AND SOLUTIONS — UNIT TEST

1. D	2. D	3. C

1. D

Choice D is correct. The question Ryan most likely asked was, "Which day of the week do you like best?"

From Ryan's data, he wrote down four days of the week. The only question that would have days of the week as answers is "Which day of the week do you like best?"

2. D

Step 1
Compare the heights of the bars for each type of pet.

1. The bar for cats (7) is lower than the bar for dogs (9).
2. The bar for cats (7) is higher than the bar for hamsters (3).
3. The bar for guinea pigs (2) is higher than the bar for turtles (1).
4. The bar for hamsters (3) is higher than the bar for guinea pigs (2).

Step 2
Determine which statement is true.

Since the bar for hamsters is higher than the bar for guinea pigs, hamsters are more popular than guinea pigs.

3. C

Step 1
Determine the number of votes each project received.

Juice box recycling received 16 votes.
Worm composting received 8 votes.
Car-pooling to school received 2 votes.
Picking up garbage received 4 votes.

Step 2
Arrange the projects from least to greatest.

Since car-pooling to school received the least amount of votes (2), the order is car-pooling to school, then picking up garbage (4), then worm composting (8), and finally, juice box recycling (16).

KEY Strategies for Success on Tests

AN OVERVIEW OF THE TEST

This section is all about the skills and strategies you need to be successful on the Alberta Mathematics 3 Provincial Achievement Test. It is designed for you to use together with your classroom learning and assignments.

Finding Out About the Test

Here are some questions you may wish to discuss with your teacher to help you prepare for the Alberta Mathematics 3 Provincial Achievement Test.

1.	What will this test assess, or cover?	The test assesses the expectations from 4 math units: Number, Patterns and Relations, Shape and Space, and Statistics and Probability. The questions will test your ability to understand and apply the science concepts you have learned throughout the year.
2.	What materials do I need to bring to write the test?	You need a pencil and an eraser.
3.	Can I use a calculator during the test?	Students may use manipulative materials when completing the test, but may not use a calculator.
4.	Are there any materials provided for the test?	No
5.	What kinds of questions are on the test?	The test has 40 multiple-choice questions that are worth one point each.
6.	How much time do I have to write the test?	You will have 2 hours to complete the test, with an additional 30 minutes provided if necessary.
7.	How important is this test to my final grade?	Your teacher can answer this question.

Having a good understanding of effective test taking skills can help you do well on the test. Being familiar with the question format may help you in preparing for quizzes, unit tests, or year-end tests.

This section is all about the skills and strategies you need to be successful on tests. It is designed for you to use together with your classroom learning and assignments.

TEST PREPARATION AND TEST-TAKING SKILLS

THINGS TO CONSIDER WHEN TAKING A TEST

- It is normal to feel anxious before you write a test. You can manage this anxiety by
  - thinking positive thoughts. Imagine yourself doing well on the test.
  - making a conscious effort to relax by taking several slow, deep, controlled breaths. Concentrate on the air going in and out of your body.

- Before you begin the test, ask questions if you are unsure of anything.

- Jot down key words or phrases from any instructions your teacher gives you.

- Look over the entire test to find out the number and kinds of questions on the test.

- Read each question closely and reread if necessary.

- Pay close attention to key vocabulary words. Sometimes these are **bolded** or *italicized*, and they are usually important words in the question.

- If you are putting your answers on an answer sheet, mark your answers carefully. Always print clearly. If you wish to change an answer, erase the mark completely and then ensure your final answer is darker than the one you have erased.

- Use highlighting to note directions, key words, and vocabulary that you find confusing or that are important to answering the question.

- Double-check to make sure you have answered everything before handing in your test.

When taking tests, students often overlook the easy words. Failure to pay close attention to these words can result in an incorrect answer. One way to avoid this is to be aware of these words and to underline, circle, or highlight them while you are taking the test.

Even though some words are easy to understand, they can change the meaning of the entire question, so it is important that you pay attention to them. Here are some examples.

all	always	most likely	probably	best	not
difference	usually	except	most	unlikely	likely

Example

1. Which of the following equations is **not** correct?

    A. $3 + 2 = 5$

    B. $4 - 3 = 1$

    C. $5 \times 4 = 15$

    D. $6 \times 3 = 18$

HELPFUL STRATEGIES FOR ANSWERING MULTIPLE-CHOICE QUESTIONS

A multiple-choice question gives you some information, and then asks you to select an answer from four choices. Each question has one correct answer. The other answers are distractors, which are incorrect. Below are some strategies to help you when answering multiple-choice questions.

- Quickly skim through the entire test. Find out how many questions there are and plan your time accordingly.

- Read and reread questions carefully. Underline key words and try to think of an answer before looking at the choices.

- If there is a graphic, look at the graphic, read the question, and go back to the graphic. Then, you may want to underline the important information from the question.

- Carefully read the choices. Read the question first and then each answer that goes with it.

- When choosing an answer, try to eliminate those choices that are clearly wrong or do not make sense.

- Some questions may ask you to select the best answer. These questions will always include words like *best*, *most appropriate*, or *most likely*. All of the answers will be correct to some degree, but one of the choices will be better than the others in some way. Carefully read all four choices before choosing the answer you think is the best.

- If you do not know the answer, or if the question does not make sense to you, it is better to guess than to leave it blank.

- Do not spend too much time on any one question. Make a mark (*) beside a difficult question and come back to it later. If you are leaving a question to come back to later, make sure you also leave the space on the answer sheet, if you are using one.

- Remember to go back to the difficult questions at the end of the test; sometimes clues are given throughout the test that will provide you with answers.

- Note any negative words like *no* or *not* and be sure your choice fits the question.

- Before changing an answer, be sure you have a very good reason to do so.

- Do not look for patterns on your answer sheet, if you are using one.

HELPFUL STRATEGIES FOR ANSWERING OPEN-RESPONSE QUESTIONS

A written response requires you to respond to a question or directive such as **explain**, **predict**, **list**, **describe**, **show your work**, **solve**, or **calculate**. In preparing for open-response tasks you may wish to:

- Read and reread the question carefully.
- Recognize and pay close attention to directing words such as *explain*, *show your work*, and *describe*.
- Underline key words and phrases that indicate what is required in your answer, such as *explain*, *estimate*, *answer*, *calculate*, or *show your work*.
- Write down rough, point-form notes regarding the information you want to include in your answer.
- Think about what you want to say and organize information and ideas in a coherent and concise manner within the time limit you have for the question.
- Be sure to answer every part of the question that is asked.
- Include as much information as you can when you are asked to explain your thinking.
- Include a picture or diagram if it will help to explain your thinking.
- Try to put your final answer to a problem in a complete sentence to be sure it is reasonable.
- Reread your response to ensure you have answered the question.
- Think: Does your answer make sense?
- Listen: Does it sound right?
- Use appropriate subject vocabulary and terms in your response.

What You Need to Know about Mathematics Tests

To do well on a mathematics test, you need to understand and apply your knowledge of mathematical concepts. Reading skills can also make a difference in how well you perform. Reading skills can help you follow instructions and find key words, as well as read graphs, diagrams, and tables. They can also help you solve mathematics problems.

Mathematics tests usually have two types of questions: questions that ask for understanding of mathematics ideas and questions that test how well you can solve mathematics problems.

How You Can Prepare for the Mathematics Test

Below are some strategies that are particular to preparing for and writing mathematics tests.

- Know how to use your calculator and, if it is allowed, use your own for the test.
- Note-taking is a good way to review and study important information from your class notes and textbook.
- Sketch a picture of the problem, procedure, or term. Drawing is helpful for learning and remembering concepts.
- Check your answer to practice questions by working backward to the beginning. You can find the beginning by going step-by-step in reverse order.
- When answering questions with graphics (pictures, diagrams, tables, or graphs), read the test question carefully.
  - Read the title of the graphic and any key words.
  - Read the test question carefully to figure out what information you need to find in the graphic.
  - Go back to the graphic to find the information you need.
- Decide which operation is needed.
- Always pay close attention when pressing the keys on your calculator. Repeat the procedure a second time to be sure you pressed the correct keys.

TEST PREPARATION COUNTDOWN

If you develop a plan for studying and test preparation, you will perform well on tests.

Here is a general plan to follow seven days before you write a test.

Countdown: 7 Days before the Test

1. Use "Finding Out About the Test" to help you make your own personal test preparation plan.

2. Review the following information:
   – areas to be included on the test

   – types of test items

   – general and specific test tips

3. Start preparing for the test at least 7 days before the test. Develop your test preparation plan and set time aside to prepare and study.

Countdown: 6, 5, 4, 3, 2 Days before the Test

1. Review old homework assignments, quizzes, and tests.

2. Rework problems on quizzes and tests to make sure you still know how to solve them.

3. Correct any errors made on quizzes and tests.

4. Review key concepts, processes, formulas, and vocabulary.

5. Create practice test questions for yourself and then answer them. Work out many sample problems.

Countdown: The Night before the Test

1. The night before the test is for final preparation, which includes reviewing and gathering material needed for the test before going to bed.

2. Most important is getting a good night's rest and knowing you have done everything possible to do well on the test.

Test Day

1. Eat a healthy and nutritious breakfast.

2. Ensure you have all the necessary materials.

3. Think positive thoughts: "I can do this." "I am ready." "I know I can do well."

4. Arrive at your school early so you are not rushing, which can cause you anxiety and stress.

SUMMARY OF HOW TO BE SUCCESSFUL DURING A TEST

You may find some of the following strategies useful for writing a test.

- Take two or three deep breaths to help you relax.
- Read the directions carefully and underline, circle, or highlight any important words.
- Look over the entire test to understand what you will need to do.
- Budget your time.
- Begin with an easy question, or a question you know you can answer correctly, rather than following the numerical question order of the test.
- If you cannot remember how to answer a question, try repeating the deep breathing and physical relaxation activities first. Then, move on to visualization and positive self-talk to get yourself going.
- When answering a question with graphics (pictures, diagrams, tables, or graphs), look at the question carefully.
  - Read the title of the graphic and any key words.
  - Read the test question carefully to figure out what information you need to find in the graphic.
  - Go back to the graphic to find the information you need.
- Write down anything you remember about the subject on the reverse side of your test paper. This activity sometimes helps to remind you that you do know something and you are capable of writing the test.
- Look over your test when you have finished and double-check your answers to be sure you did not forget anything.

Practice Test

PRACTICE TEST

Use the following information to answer the next question.

Liam starts at 634 and correctly skip counts forward by 100s.

1. Which of the following numbers will Liam say while he is counting?
   A. 534 B. 644

   C. 700 D. 734

Use the following information to answer the next question.

Adam bounces a ball 50 times in a row.

2. In words, the number 50 is written as
   A. five B. fifty

   C. fivty D. fivety

Use the following information to answer the next question.

Jamaal used these base ten blocks to build a number.

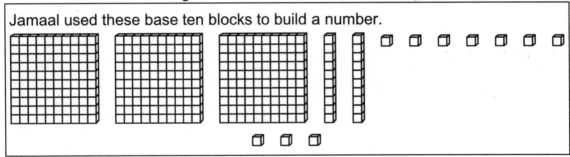

3. What number did Jamaal build?
   A. 309 B. 320 330

   C. 330 D. 339

4. Which of the following numbers has a value less than 875?
   A. 885 B. 869

   C. 881 D. 879

Use the following information to answer the next question.

To estimate the number of jellybeans in a jar, Molly fills a little cup with 10 jellybeans and uses it as a referent.

10

5. A good estimate for Molly to make is
   A. 200

   C. 80

   B. 120

   D. 50

6. In the number 408, the zero is in the
   A. ones place

   C. hundreds place

   B. tens place

   D. thousands place

Use the following information to answer the next question.

Brad shows the number 232 as 2 hundreds, 3 tens, and 2 ones.

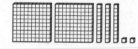

7. The number 232 can also be shown as
   A. 1 hundred, 2 tens, and 12 ones

   C. 2 hundreds, 3 tens, and 10 ones

   B. 1 hundred, 13 tens, and 2 ones

   D. 2 hundreds, 3 tens, and 12 ones

8. Jay correctly adds 78 + 12 in his head. Which of the following mental strategies did he **most likely** use?
   A. 7 + 8 + 1 + 2

   C. 70 + 10 + 10

   B. 70 + 10 + 12

   D. 70 + 80 + 12

Use the following information to answer the next question.

> In Red Deer, 65 people got on an empty bus. The bus then drove to Calgary. In Calgary, 32 people got off the bus. Marie wants to know how many people stayed on the bus.

9. Which of the following mental strategies could Marie use to solve this problem?

   A. 65 + 32

   C. 32 + 32 + 1

   B. 32 + 8 + 15

   D. 60 – 30 and 5 + 2

Use the following information to answer the next question.

> There were 94 people shopping at a toy store. At 5 o'clock in the evening, 63 people were still at the store.

10. About how many people left the store before 5 o'clock?

    A. 10

    C. 30

    B. 15

    D. 45

Use the following information to answer the next question.

> This chart shows the number of students that went on a field trip and the number that did not.

Grades 1, 2, and 3		Grades 4, 5, and 6	
Number of students on the field trip	Number of students not on the field trip	Number of students on the field trip	Number of students not on the field trip
252	18	346	32

11. How many students in total went on the field trip?

    A. 270

    C. 598

    B. 348

    D. 648

12. David wants to add 28 + 34 by using the strategy of making a ten. Which of the following numbers should he add?

    A. 20 + 32

    C. 30 + 32

    B. 20 + 36

    D. 30 + 36

Use the following information to answer the next question.

Joel makes arrays out of tiles to show multiplication facts.

13. Which of the following arrays shows 4 × 3?

A.

B.

C.

D.

Use the following information to answer the next question.

21 − 7 = 14, 14 − 7 = 7, 7 − 7 = 0

14. The given repeated subtraction equation represents which of the following division sentences?

   A. 21 ÷ 2

   B. 21 ÷ 3

   C. 21 ÷ 4

   D. 21 ÷ 7

Use the following information to answer the next question.

A diagram of a circle is given.

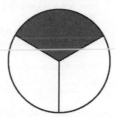

15. Which of the following fractions represents the shaded part of the circle?

   A. $\dfrac{2}{2}$

   B. $\dfrac{2}{3}$

   C. $\dfrac{1}{2}$

   D. $\dfrac{1}{3}$

16. The shaded part of which of the following circles shows a fraction greater than $\frac{4}{10}$ and less than $\frac{7}{10}$?

A.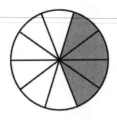

B.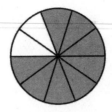

C.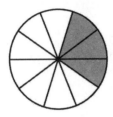

D.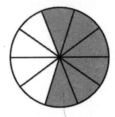

17. Which of the following number patterns has the pattern rule of "Start at 8 and add 8 each time"?

  A. 8, 16, 24, 32   B. 8, 16, 32, 64

  C. 8, 16, 28, 36   D. 8, 18, 28, 38

Use the following information to answer the next question.

Mrs. Richards showed Mike the following number pattern:
_____, _____, 131, 141, 151, 161

18. What are the missing numbers in the number pattern?

  A. 111 and 121   B. 101 and 111

  C. 101 and 121   D. 100 and 121

Use the following information to answer the next question.

Amy wanted to sort these buttons. She sorted them by dark or light and by one hole or two holes.

19. Which of the following charts shows the buttons sorted correctly?

A.

	Dark	Light
One hole		
Two holes		

B.

	Dark	Light
One hole		
Two holes		

C.

	Dark	Light
One hole		
Two holes		

D.

	Dark	Light
One hole		
Two holes		

Use the following information to answer the next question.

Su-Ling loves cats. She has 5 posters of cats on her bedroom walls. After her birthday party last night, she now has 20 posters.

In the number sentence 5 + *P* = 20, *P* represents the number of cat posters that Su-Ling got for her birthday.

20. What is the missing number in the equation?

A. *P* = 4   B. *P* = 5

C. *P* = 10   D. *P* = 15

Use the following information to answer the next question.

One Saturday afternoon, Daria and two friends played dress-up in Daria's bedroom while their mothers visited. After the friends went home, Daria's mother asked her to clean up her room.

21. Which of the following units is the **best** measure of how long it would most likely take Daria to clean up her room?

A. Seconds   B. Minutes

C. Weeks   D. Days

Use the following information to answer the next question.

Lucy the elephant can drink 10 L of water every 20 minutes.

22. How many litres of water could Lucy drink in 1 hour?

A. 10 L   B. 20 L

C. 30 L   D. 40 L

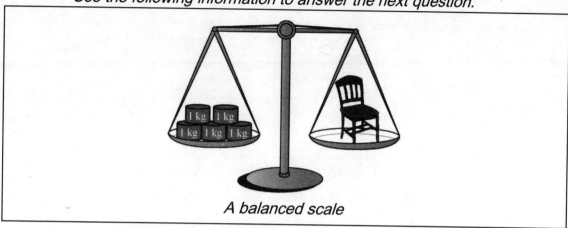

A balanced scale

23. What is the mass of the chair in grams?

A. 5 g

B. 50 g

C. 500 g

D. 5 000 g

Use the following information to answer the next question.

Sharla put a 1 kg weight on one side of a scale.

24. Which of the following objects should Sharla put on the other side of the scale in order to balance it?

A. A glue bottle

B. A math textbook

C. A box of pencil crayons

D. A package of three scribblers

Use the following information to answer the next question.

Carol measures the length of this rectangle. The rectangle's length is two times longer than its width.

4 cm

25. What is the perimeter of the rectangle?

A. 6 cm

B. 8 cm

C. 12 cm

D. 16 cm

Practice TEST

Use the following information to answer the next question.

Essa drew these four shapes on centimetre grid paper.

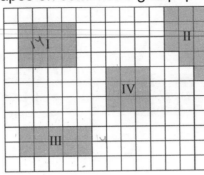

26. Which two of the shapes have the same perimeter?
   A. Shapes I and II   B. Shapes II and III
   C. Shapes I and III   D. Shapes II and IV

27. Which of the following figures has five faces, nine edges, and six vertices?
   A.    B.

   C. 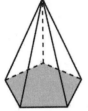   D.

Use the following information to answer the next question.

Allie sorts some shapes into two groups. Group A contains shapes in which all the sides are the same length. Group B contains shapes in which all the sides are not the same length.

28. Which of the following charts shows how Allie sorted the shapes?

A.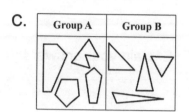

B.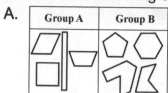

C.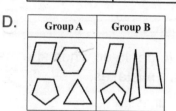

D.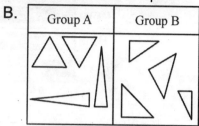

Use the following information to answer the next question.

Jackson surveyed students in his school to see which one of six summer sports they liked the most. He put his data into this chart.

Favourite Sport

Sport	Number of Students
Baseball	ﬤ ﬤ | | | |
Basketball	ﬤ ﬤ ﬤ ﬤ
Biking	ﬤ ﬤ ﬤ
Rollerblading	ﬤ ﬤ ﬤ | | |
Soccer	ﬤ ﬤ | | | |
Swimming	ﬤ ﬤ ﬤ ﬤ |

29. Which of the following conclusions **cannot** be drawn from the data shown in the chart?

A. Biking is less popular than rollerblading.

B. Rollerblading is the fourth most popular sport.

C. Playing soccer is as popular as playing baseball.

D. Playing soccer is one of the least favorite sports.

Use the following information to answer the next question.

Ella surveyed all the students in two Grade 3 classes to see what colour eyes they had. She made this graph to show the data she collected.

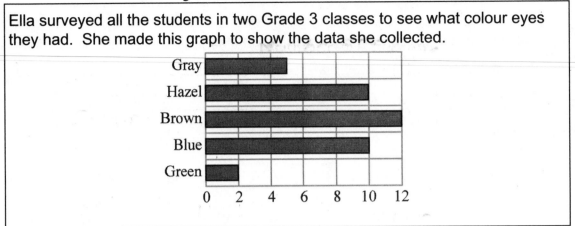

Written Response

30. What did Ella forget to do when she made her graph? Explain your answer by correcting Ella's mistakes.

ANSWERS AND SOLUTIONS — PRACTICE TEST

1.	D	7.	B	13.	D	19.	A	25.	C
2.	B	8.	C	14.	D	20.	D	26.	C
3.	C	9.	C	15.	D	21.	B	27.	D
4.	B	10.	C	16.	D	22.	C	28.	D
5.	B	11.	C	17.	A	23.	D	29.	B
6.	B	12.	C	18.	A	24.	B	30.	WR

1. D

Step 1
Understand the pattern.

- When counting by 100s, the digits in the tens and ones places (3 and 4) must stay the same.
- When counting forward, the digit in the hundreds place must be more than 6.

Step 2
Find the number that fits the pattern.
The number 734 ends in 34, and the digit 7 is more than 6.
The number Liam will say is 734.

2. B

To write the number 50 in words, drop the –ve from the word five (5), and add the letters –fty to the end of the word.
five → fifty

In words, the number 50 is written as fifty.

3. C

Step 1
Find the value of each set of blocks.

- The 3 hundred flats have a value of 300.
- The 2 ten rods have a value of 20.
- The 10 units have a value of 10.

Step 2
Add the values of the blocks together.
300 + 20 + 10 = 330
The number that Jamaal built is 330.

4. B

Step 1
Compare the hundreds.
885
869
881
879
All four numbers have 8 hundreds.
Move to the right, and compare the tens.

Step 2
Compare the tens.
885
869
881
879
Both 885 and 881 have 8 tens, so they have greater values than 875 because 875 has 7 tens.
Move to the right, and compare the ones.

Step 3
Compare the ones.
Both 879 and 875 have 7 tens, but 879 has more ones than 875, so it has a greater value.
879
875
That means that 869, with 6 tens, has a value that is less than 875.

5. B

Step 1
Figure out how many cups will cover the jar.
About 12 cups will cover the jar.

Step 2
Make the estimate.
Count by 10s for each of the 12 cups drawn.
10, 20, 30, 40, 50, 60, 70, 80, 90, 100, 110, 120
A good estimate for Molly to make is that there are about 120 jellybeans in the jar.

6. B

In the number 408, there are 4 hundreds and 8 ones.

The zero is in the tens place. It acts as a placeholder because there are no tens in 408.

7. B

Step 1
Regroup one of the hundreds into 10 tens.
You now have 1 hundred.

Step 2
Add the 10 tens to the 3 tens.
10 + 3 = 13
You now have 13 tens.
The ones stay the same.
The number 232 can also be shown as 1 hundred, 13 tens, and 2 ones.

8. C

Jay most likely used the strategy of adding from left to right.
78 → 70 + 8
12 → 10 + 2

Add the tens.
70 + 10

Add the ones.
8 + 2 = 10

Add the tens and ones together.
70 + 10 + 10 = 90

9. C

To find how many people stayed on the bus, you need to subtract 65 – 32.

To solve this problem in your head, you can use doubles.

Think of 32 + ⬚32 = 64 and 64 + ⬚1 = 65.

Now, add 32 and 1.
⬚32 + ⬚1 = 33

So, 65 – 32 = 33.

10. C

Step 1
Use front-end estimation.
Keep the front-end digit, and replace the digits on the right with zeros.
94 → 90
63 → 60
To subtract 94 – 63 using estimation, use 90 – 60.

Step 2
Subtract the two numbers.
90 – 60 = 30
About 30 people left the toy store before 5 o'clock in the evening.

11. C

Choice C is correct. In total, 598 students went on the field trip.

To find the total number of students that went on the field trip, add the number of students that went in grades 1 to 3 and grades 4 to 6.

252 (grades 1 to 3)
+346 (grades 4 to 6)
598

The number of students from grades 1 to 6 that went on the field trip was 598.

12. C

When you use the strategy of making a ten, begin by changing the number that is closest to a multiple of 10.

In 28 + 34, the 28 is closest to 30, which is a multiple of 10. To change 28 into 30, you need to add 2.

You then take that 2 away from the 34, so the 34 will become 32.

To find the final answer, add 30 and 32.
28 + 34 = ?
30 + 32 = 62

13. D

Figure out what each digit in 4 × 3 stands for.

One of the digits will stand for the number of rows, and the other digit will stand for the number in each row.

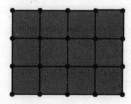

This array shows 3 rows of tiles with 4 tiles in each row.

14. D

The repeated subtraction shows 7 being subtracted from 21 until the answer is 0.

The division sentence represented by the repeated subtraction is 21 ÷ 7.

15. D

Step 1
Determine the denominator.
Since the circle is divided into three equal parts, the denominator is 3.

$\dfrac{?}{3}$

Step 2
Determine the numerator.
Since one part is shaded, the numerator is 1.

$\dfrac{1}{3}$

The fraction that represents the shaded part of the circle is $\dfrac{1}{3}$.

16. D

Since the denominators are all the same, compare the numerators.

To be greater than 4 and less than 7, 5 or 6 parts must be shaded.
4, 5, 6, 7

This circle has 6 of the 10 parts shaded.

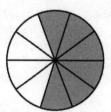

The fraction $\dfrac{6}{10}$ is greater than $\dfrac{4}{10}$ and less than $\dfrac{7}{10}$.

17. A

Choice A is correct. The number pattern that follows the rule is 8, 16, 24, 32:

(8 + 8 = 16), (16 + 8 = 24), (24 + 8 = 32)

18. **A**

The missing numbers in the number pattern are 111 and 121.

The 1s and 100s digits stay the same, so the number pattern is counting by 10s.

Start on the right side (161), and move to the left. Subtract 10 each time (count backward by 10s).

Continue subtracting by 10 or counting backward by 10s to find the first two numbers of the pattern.

(131 – 10 = 121)(121 – 10 = 111)

19. **A**

Step 1
Sort the buttons by color.
Put the dark buttons together. Put the light buttons together.

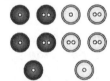

Step 2
Sort the buttons by the number of holes.

- Put the dark buttons with one hole in the top left box.
- Put the light buttons with one hole in the top right box.
- Put the dark buttons with two holes in the bottom left box.
- Put the light buttons with two holes in the bottom right box.

This chart shows the buttons sorted correctly.

	Dark	Light
One hole	● ●●	○ ○
Two holes	●● ●●	○ ○ ○

20. **D**

Choice D posters foD

$5 + P = 20$

The 5 posters that Su-Ling has on her bedroom walls plus the number of posters that she got for her birthday (P) equal the total number of posters (20).

Because subtraction is the opposite operation of addition, subtract 5 from 20 to find what number P represents.

$5 + P = 20$
$P = 20 – 5$
$P = 15$
$5 + 15 = 20$

The value of P is 15.

21. **B**

Step 1
Examine each option given.
Seconds are very small units of time.
No matter how small the room, it would take more than a few seconds to clean.
Minutes are a longer unit of time.
Depending on how messy the room is, most rooms can be cleaned in minutes.
Days are long units of time. There are 24 hours in a day. No matter how messy the room is, it should not take days to clean.
Weeks are the longest unit of time.
There are 7 days in a week. It would not take weeks to clean a room.

Step 2
Identify the best unit of measure.
Daria and her friends were probably playing dress-up for a few hours. In this case, minutes is the best unit of time to use when measuring how long it would take her to clean up her room.

22. **C**

Lucy can drink 10 L of water in 20 minutes.
There are 60 minutes in 1 hour.
20 min + 20 min + 20 min = 60 min

Since there are three sets of 20 minutes in 1 hour, Lucy will drink 10 L three times.
10 L + 10 L + 10 L = 30 L

In 1 hour, Lucy will drink 30 L.

23. **D**

Step 1

Determine the mass of the weights on the left side of the scale.

There are five weights, and each weight has a mass of 1 kg.

Add 1 kg + 1 kg + 1 kg+1 kg + 1 kg = 5 kg, or multiply 1 kg × 5.

The mass of the five weights is 5 kg.

Step 2

Determine the mass of the chair.

Since the scale is balanced, the mass of the chair is the same as the mass of the five weights.

The mass of the chair is 5 kg.

Step 3

Change kilograms to grams.
1 kg = 1 000 g

Make a chart to help you determine the number of grams in 5 kg.

Kilograms	Grams
1	1 000
2	2 000
3	3 000
4	4 000
5	5 000

The chair has a mass of 5 000 g.

24. **B**

Step 1

Think about each object.

- A glue bottle would have a mass that is less than 1 kg.
- A math textbook would have a mass that is about 1 kg.
- A box of pencil crayons would have a mass that is less than 1 kg.
- A package of three scribblers would have a mass that is less than 1 kg.

Step 2

Select the best option.

Of the objects listed, the object that would best balance the scale would be the math textbook.

25. **C**

Choice C is correct. The perimeter of this rectangle is 12 cm.

If one side of the rectangle is 4 cm long, then the opposite side is also 4 cm long.

The length is two times the width. That means the width is half of the length. $4 \div 2 = 2$

The width of the rectangle is 2 cm. The opposite side is also 2 cm.

Add all four sides together:
$4 + 4 + 2 + 2 = 12$ (Remember: You can add the numbers in any order.)

26. **C**

Choice C is correct. Shapes I and III have the same perimeter.

Shape I: $3 + 3 + 4 + 4 = 14$ cm

Shape III: $5 + 5 + 2 + 2 = 14$ cm

27. D

Step 1
Count the number of faces, edges, and vertices in each figure.

The rectangular prism has six faces, twelve edges, and eight vertices.

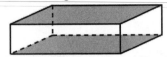

The rectangular-based pyramid has five faces, eight edges, and five vertices.

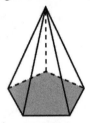

The pentagonal pyramid has six faces, ten edges, and six vertices.

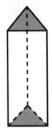

The triangular prism has five faces, nine edges, and six vertices.

Step 2
Identify the figure with five faces, nine edges, and six vertices.
The triangular prism has five faces, nine edges, and six vertices.

28. D

Step 1
Examine the side lengths of each shape in the group A chart.
The only chart that has shapes with equal side lengths in group A is this one:

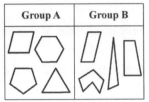

Step 2
Examine the side lengths of the shapes in group B in this chart.
None of the four shapes in group B in this chart have equal side lengths.

29. B

Choice B is correct. The conclusion that cannot be drawn from the chart is that rollerblading is the fourth most popular sport.

Rollerblading has the third highest number of votes, so it is the third most popular sport not the fourth most popular sport.

Swimming: 21

Basketball: 20

Rollerblading: 18

Biking: 15

Baseball and soccer: 14

30. WR

Makes a connection between displaying data and using appropriate labels/titles, giving a highly effective explanation and examples.
E.g., Ella forgot the title and the labels.
Title – Eye Colours in Two Grade 3 Classes
Horizontal axis – Number of students
Vertical axis – Eye colour

Appendices

Addition Table

+	0	1	2	3	4	5	6	7	8	9
0	0	1	2	3	4	5	6	7	8	9
1	1	2	3	4	5	6	7	8	9	10
2	2	3	4	5	6	7	8	9	10	11
3	3	4	5	6	7	8	9	10	11	12
4	4	5	6	7	8	9	10	11	12	13
5	5	6	7	8	9	10	11	12	13	14
6	6	7	8	9	10	11	12	13	14	15
7	7	8	9	10	11	12	13	14	15	16
8	8	9	10	11	12	13	14	15	16	17
9	9	10	11	12	13	14	15	16	17	18

Hundreds Chart

1	2	3	4	5	6	7	8	9	10
11	12	13	14	15	16	17	18	19	20
21	22	23	24	25	26	27	28	29	30
31	32	33	34	35	36	37	38	39	40
41	42	43	44	45	46	47	48	49	50
51	52	53	54	55	56	57	58	59	60
61	62	63	64	65	66	67	68	69	70
71	72	73	74	75	76	77	78	79	80
81	82	83	84	85	86	87	88	89	90
91	92	93	94	95	96	97	98	99	100

NUMBER LINES

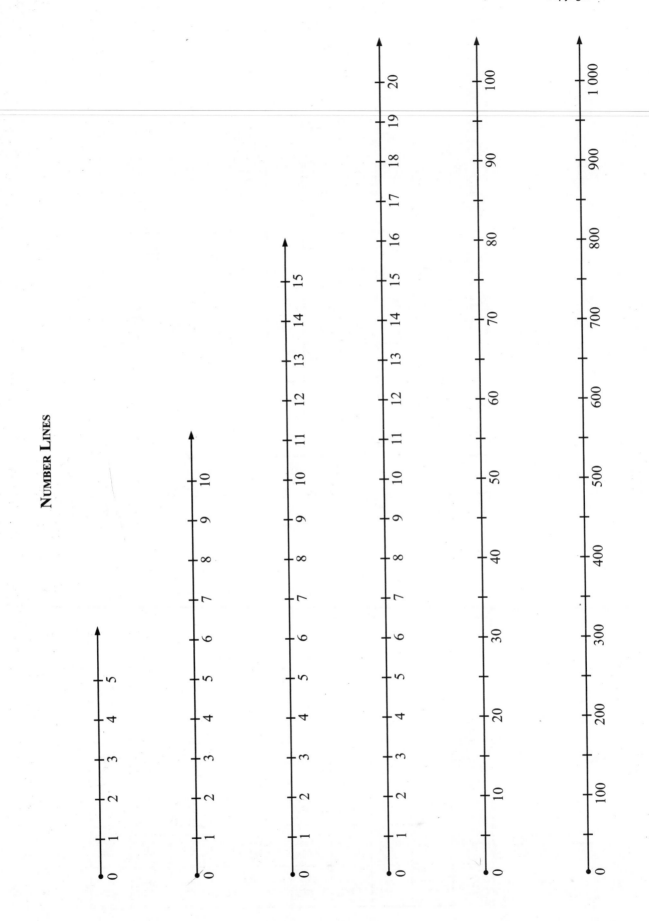

Castle Rock Research, the creator of **The KEY** and the **SNAP Workbook**, has developed a new online study tool: **SOLARO**.

SOLARO - Student Oriented Learning, Assessment, and Reporting Online - is a grades 3-12 learning resource for math, science, and English language arts accessible both online and on mobile devices. **SOLARO** provides age-appropriate, curriculum-aligned lessons, activities, exercises, and quizzes with detailed solutions. Content, in the form of text, graphics, and multimedia is available 24 hours a day in a well-organized and highly engaging system.

SOLARO was designed by educators to respond to the needs of the three major stakeholders in education: students, parents, and teachers.

SOLARO's teacher interface makes it easy to manage a full suite of classes and students. The user-friendly system allows teachers to add classes and to populate them with students with just a click of the mouse.

Teachers can easily view all their course content, as well as the specific curriculum standards linked to each lesson. Educators can be confident that relevant content is covered in detail, as most curriculum standards have multiple lessons attached to them. Teachers can also use the playlist feature to add in their own customized content, including documents, media, and web links.

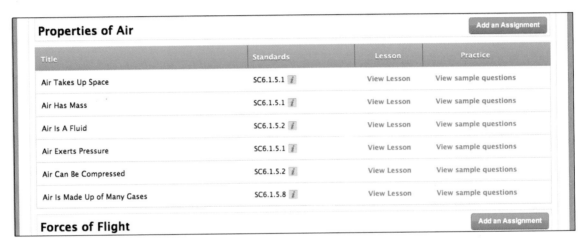

With the assignment generator feature in **SOLARO,** teachers can assemble customized assignments with problems selected from an extensive database of educator-reviewed questions automatically sorted by subject, topic, and lesson. Teachers manage student access to any given assignment, controlling the time available for completing each assignment. These assignments may be provided to students digitally or in print.

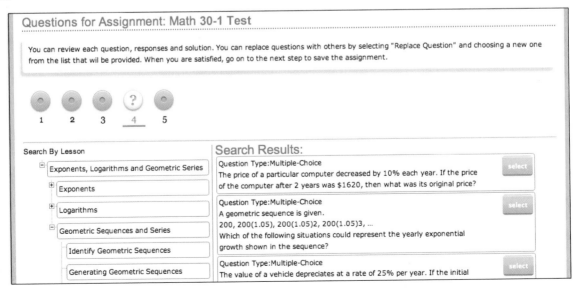

Immediate scoring and reporting enables teachers to track performance and helps them to determine if further instruction or remediation may be needed at the individual or class level. Class results can be anonymously displayed on a whiteboard for class-wide review.

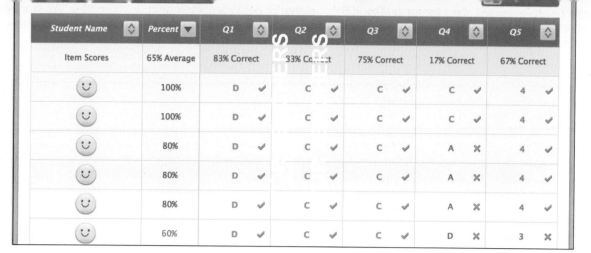

Teachers can view progress reports for every student, detailing the student's achievements by date completed, lessons viewed, practice quizzes taken, and assessment results. The assessment results link individual questions to the related curriculum standards, showing the student's areas strength and weakness in great detail. The tools in **SOLARO** benefit teachers by reducing much of the time usually spent in planning, preparing, grading, and reporting.

SOLARO provides a secure and guided online environment for students as they study, work through exercises, and take assessments. The home screen encourages good study habits by providing a customizable, ordered to-do list and an overview of previously completed assessments and quizzes.

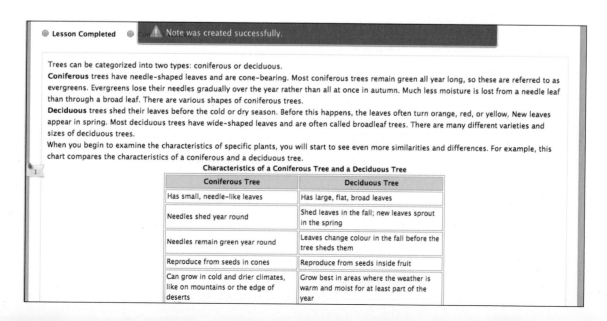

While viewing an individual lesson, students can easily create notes and flashcards for future studying. Notes and flashcards are linked to the original lesson and assembled under a separate tab, sorted by subject. Peer tutoring is also built into the lessons by a monitored discussion board shared by all **SOLARO** users.

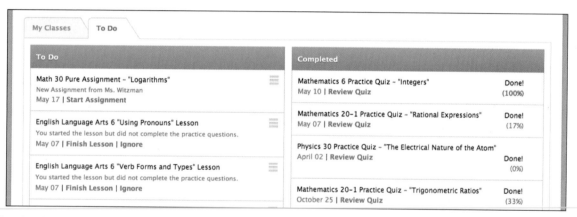

Students are awarded stars for each lesson they review or every assessment they complete. As students accumulate stars, they can use them to purchase rewards to build a personalized avatar. This provides incentive by providing a fun, interactive, motivational reward for participation and success.

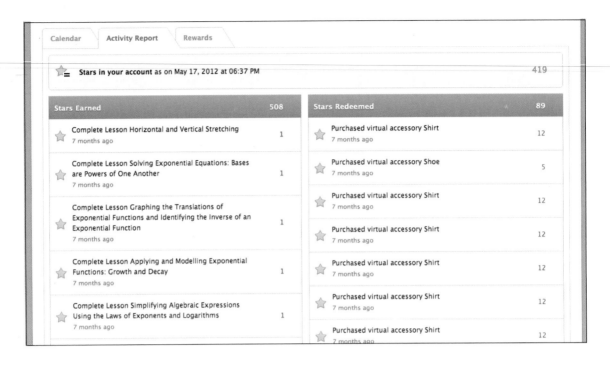

All progress is saved instantly so students can access pick up their mobile devices and continue where they left off on their home computers.

The **SOLARO** parent interface allows parents to monitor the individual progress for each of their children, and it provides detailed reports for each child's account. These easy to read reports show how many activities have been completed, when they were reported, the progress of the student through their courses, the level of achievement on tests and assignments, and deficiencies that may need to be addressed. Parents can configure reports to automatically send to their mobile devices.

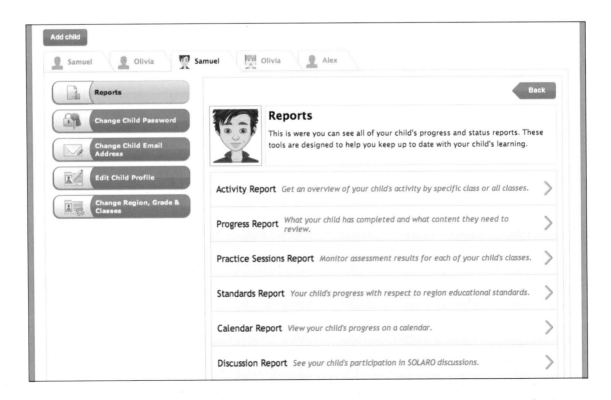

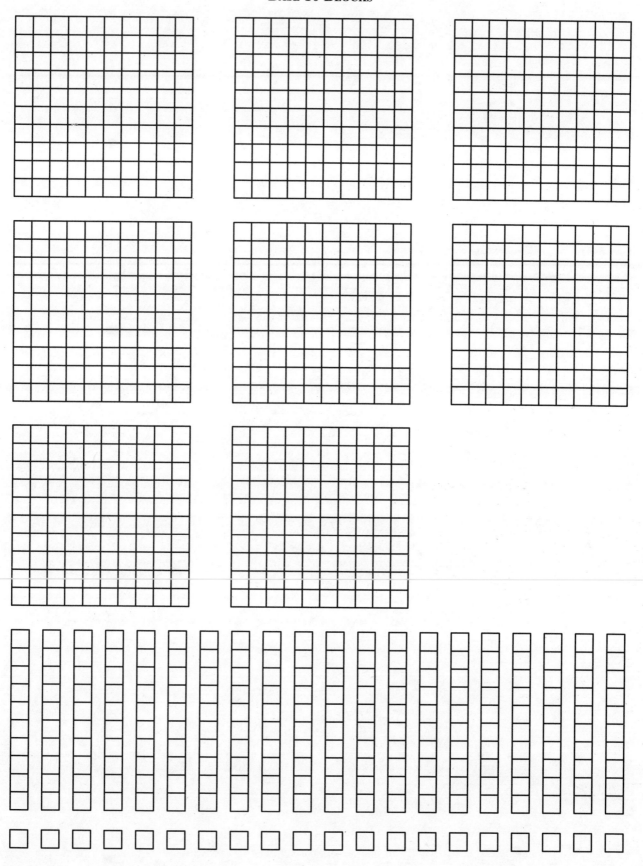

100s Grid

FRACTION STRIPS

1					
$\frac{1}{2}$		$\frac{2}{2}$			
$\frac{1}{3}$		$\frac{2}{3}$		$\frac{3}{3}$	

| $\frac{1}{4}$ | $\frac{2}{4}$ | $\frac{3}{4}$ | $\frac{4}{4}$ |

| $\frac{1}{5}$ | $\frac{2}{5}$ | $\frac{3}{5}$ | $\frac{4}{5}$ | $\frac{5}{5}$ |

| $\frac{1}{10}$ | $\frac{2}{10}$ | $\frac{3}{10}$ | $\frac{4}{10}$ | $\frac{5}{10}$ | $\frac{6}{10}$ | $\frac{7}{10}$ | $\frac{8}{10}$ | $\frac{9}{10}$ | $\frac{10}{10}$ |

GLOSSARY

array
> Items or objects arranged in rows and columns.

base
> The shape of the face used to name the 3-D object.

data
> A collection of information or facts.

decreasing pattern
> A sequence or design that shrinks or becomes smaller.

digit
> Any of the numbers 0, 1, 2, 3, 4, 5, 6, 7, 8, or 9.

edge
> The straight line formed where two faces of a three-dimensional figure meet.

equation
> A number sentence using an equal sign (=) to show both sides have the same value.

estimate
> An educated guess of a number, calculation, quantity, or measurment.

face
> Any surface of a solid.

graph
> A visual representation of data.

increasing pattern
> A sequence or design that grows or becomes bigger.

irregular polygon
> A two-dimensional closed figure whose sides are not the same length and whose angles are not all congruent.

Mass
> The amount of matter in an object.

mental strategy
> A plan (method) that can help solve problems in your head instead of using paper and pencil or a calculator.

pattern rule
> A statement that explains or tells how to make a pattern.

polygon

A closed two-dimensional figure made of three or more line segments. For example, a triangle, a quadrilateral, a pentagon, or an octagon.

prism

A solid formed by two congruent and parallel sides and other faces that are parallelograms.

pyramid

A solid with one face that is a polygon (the base) and triangular faces that share a common vertex.

referent

An object that has about the same size and shape as a particular measurement.

regroup

Exchanging amounts of an equal value to rename a number. For example, 4 ten rods and 12 units can be regrouped to 5 ten rods and 2 units. Both have a value of 52.

regular polygon

A polygon in which all the sides and angles are equal.

strategy

A plan to solve a problem.

vertex

The point where at least three edges meet.

CREDITS

Every effort has been made to provide proper acknowledgement of the original source and to comply with copyright law. However, some attempts to establish original copyright ownership may have been unsuccessful. If copyright ownership can be identified, please notify Castle Rock Research Corp so that appropriate corrective action can be taken.

Some images in this document are from www.clipart.com, copyright © 2011 Jupiterimages Corporation.

NOTES

So I hate this book 🙁

NOTES

NOTES

NOTES

ORDERING INFORMATION

SCHOOL ORDERS

Please contact the Learning Resource Centre (LRC) for school discount and order information.

***THE KEY* Study Guides** are specifically designed to assist students in preparing for unit tests, final exams, and provincial examinations.

***THE KEY* Study Guides**—$29.95 each plus G.S.T.

SENIOR HIGH		JUNIOR HIGH	ELEMENTARY
Biology 30	Biology 20	English Language Arts 9	English Language Arts 6
Chemistry 30	Chemistry 20	Mathematics 9	Mathematics 6
English 30-1	English 20-1	Science 9	Science 6
English 30-2	Mathematics 20-1	Social Studies 9	Social Studies 6
Mathematics 30-1	Physics 20	Mathematics 8	Mathematics 4
Mathematics 30-2	Social Studies 20-1	Mathematics 7	English Language Arts 3
Physics 30	English 10-1		Mathematics 3
Social Studies 30-1	Mathematics 10		
Social Studies 30-2	Combined		
	Science 10		
	Social Studies 10-1		

Student Notes and Problems (SNAP) Workbooks contain complete explanations of curriculum concepts, examples, and exercise questions.

SNAP Workbooks—$29.95 each plus G.S.T.

SENIOR HIGH		JUNIOR HIGH	ELEMENTARY
Biology 30	Biology 20	Mathematics 9	Mathematics 6
Chemistry 30	Chemistry 20	Science 9	Mathematics 5
Mathematics 30-1	Mathematics 20-1	Mathematics 8	Mathematics 4
Mathematics 30-2	Physics 20	Science 8	Mathematics 3
Mathematics 31	Mathematics 10	Mathematics 7	
Physics 30	Combined	Science 7	
	Science 10		

Class Notes and Problem Solved—$19.95 each plus G.S.T.

SENIOR HIGH		JUNIOR HIGH
Biology 30	Biology 20	Mathematics 9
Chemistry 30	Chemistry 20	Science 9
Mathematics 30-1	Mathematics 20-1	Mathematics 8
Mathematics 30-2	Physics 20	Science 8
Mathematics 31	Mathematics 10 Combined	Mathematics 7
Physics 30	Science 10	Science 7

Visit our website for a tour of resource content and features or order resources online at
www.castlerockresearch.com/store/

#2340, 10180 – 101 Street NW
Edmonton, AB Canada T5J 3S4
e-mail: learn@castlerockresearch.com

Phone: 780.448.9619
Toll-free: 1.800.840.6224
Fax: 780.426.3917

ORDER FORM

THE KEY	QUANTITY
Biology 30	
Chemistry 30	
English 30-1	
English 30-2	
Mathematics 30-1	
Mathematics 30-2	
Physics 30	
Biology 20	
Chemistry 20	
Social Studies 30-1	
Social Studies 30-2	
Biology 20	
Chemistry 20	
English 20-1	
Mathematics 20-1	
Physics 20	
Social Studies 20-1	
English 10-1	
Math 10 Combined	
Science 10	
Social Studies 10-1	
Social Studies 9	
English Language Arts 9	
Mathematics 9	
Science 9	
Mathematics 8	
Mathematics 7	
English Language Arts 6	
Mathematics 6	
Science 6	
Social Studies 6	
Mathematics 4	
Mathematics 3	
English Language Arts 3	

Student Notes and Problems Workbooks	QUANTITY SNAP Workbooks
Mathematics 31	
Biology 30	
Chemistry 30	
Mathematics 30-1	
Mathematics 30-2	
Physics 30	
Biology 20	
Chemistry 20	
Mathematics 20-1	
Physics 20	
Mathematics 10 Combined	
Science 10	
Mathematics 9	
Science 9	
Mathematics 8	
Science 8	
Mathematics 7	
Science 7	
Mathematics 6	
Mathematics 5	
Mathematics 4	
Mathematics 3	

Problem Solved and Class Notes	QUANTITY Solution Manuals	Class Notes	Problem Solved
Mathematics 31			
Biology 30			
Chemistry 30			
Mathematics 30-1			
Mathematics 30-2			
Physics 30			
Biology 20			
Chemistry 20			
Mathematics 20-1			
Physics 20			
Mathematics 10 Combined			
Science 10			
Mathematics 9			
Science 9			
Mathematics 8			
Science 8			
Mathematics 7			
Science 7			

Total Cost	
Subtotal 1	
Subtotal 2	
Subtotal 3	
Cost Subtotal	
Shipping and Handling*	
G.S.T	
Order Total	

CASTLE ROCK RESEARCH CORP   #2340, 10180 – 101 Street NW, Edmonton, AB T5J 3S4   **Phone:** 780.448.9619 **Fax:** 780.426.3917 **Toll-free:** 1.800.840.6224
Email: learn@castlerockresearch.com   **www.castlerockresearch.com**